CLIMATE CHANGE GOVERNANCE AT THE SUBNATIONAL GOVERNMENT LEVEL IN ASIA AND THE PACIFIC

MAY 2025

ASIAN DEVELOPMENT BANK

ADB

6 ADB Avenue, Mandaluyong City, 1550 Metro Manila, Philippines
Tel +63 2 8632 4444; Fax +63 2 8636 2444
www.adb.org

ISBN 978-92-9277-310-6 (print); 978-92-9277-311-3 (PDF); 978-92-9277-312-0 (ebook)
Publication Stock No. TCS250188
DOI: http://dx.doi.org/10.22617/TCS250188

Notes:
In this publication, "CNY" refers to yuan, "$" refers to United States dollars, "₱" refers to Philippine peso, and "₹" refers to Indian rupees.
ADB recognizes "China" as the People's Republic of China and "Vietnam" as Viet Nam.

Cover design by Madeliene Teh (photo by ADB).

Contents

Tables, Figures, and Boxes

Tables

Figures

Boxes

Acknowledgments

The preparation of this technical study on *Climate Change Governance at the Subnational Government Level in Asia and the Pacific* was led and guided by Rachana Shrestha, senior public sector specialist, Public Sector Management and Governance Sector Office, Sectors Department 3 (SG-PSMG).

We acknowledge the invaluable contributions of Preeta Lall and Gabriele (Gabe) Ferrazzi who served as drafters and authors. Additionally, insights and feedback from the peer reviewer Nisha Krishnan, climate change specialist, Climate Change, Resilience, and Environment Cluster, enhanced the quality of this publication. Review and suggestions of Joel Syquia, principal public sector specialist/knowledge team lead, SG-PSMG, are also appreciated.

Abbreviations

ADB	–	Asian Development Bank
AF	–	Adaptation Fund
Bappenas	–	Ministry of National Development Planning (Indonesia)
CIF	–	Climate Investment Funds
PRC	–	People's Republic of China
GCF	–	Green Climate Fund
GEF	–	Global Environment Facility
GHG	–	greenhouse gas
ICCTF	–	Indonesia Climate Change Trust Fund
IPCC	–	Intergovernmental Panel on Climate Change
LAPA	–	Local Adaptation Plan for Action
LCCAP	–	local climate change action plan
LGMA	–	Local Governments and Municipal Authorities
LGU	–	local government unit
LoCAL	–	Local Climate Adaptive Living Facility
MDB	–	multilateral development bank
NAP	–	National Adaptation Plan
NAPA	–	National Adaptation Programme of Action
NCDD	–	National Committee for Subnational Democratic Development
NDA	–	national designated authority
NDC	–	nationally determined contribution
OECD	–	Organisation for Economic Co-operation and Development
SAPCC	–	State Action Plan for Climate Change
SDG	–	Sustainable Development Goal
SKMCCC	–	State Knowledge Management Centre on Climate Change
SNA	–	subnational administration
SNG	–	subnational government
UNDP	–	United Nations Development Programme
UNFCCC	–	United Nations Framework Convention on Climate Change

Executive Summary

Asia and the Pacific faces significant climate change threats, making it important that all levels of government in the region join the effort to respond. The region is large, containing countries with high levels of poverty (e.g., Bangladesh and India), and many environmentally fragile areas; 13 of the world's 30 most climate-vulnerable countries are in this region. The countries in the region emit 42.4% of global greenhouse gases. This report focuses on developing economies, as these face severe challenges in financing climate change action. These countries have nonetheless made meaningful commitments through the United Nations Framework Convention on Climate Change, the Kyoto Protocol, and the Paris Agreement, and most have done so in the form of Nationally Determined Contributions (NDCs) and National Adaptation Plans. However, these efforts are falling short of adhering to the 1.5°C pathway and face difficulties in becoming operational.

Climate change action involves multiple actors, scales, and sectors. In examining the potential role of subnational governments (SNGs), it is useful to think in terms of key elements of fiscal decentralization that can expand or limit this role: functional assignment, planning and budgeting systems, revenue assignment and borrowing powers, and intergovernmental grants. These features of decentralized governance offer a lens for determining SNG roles, but any analysis must consider the diversity of SNG structures in Asia and the Pacific. Countries are divided at various scales, and can have unitary or federal structures. These factors will affect the degree of SNG autonomy that can be expected and vertical relationships.

Whatever their role and size, SNGs are becoming increasingly involved in climate change action. Their role is increasingly acknowledged in global agreements (the Paris Agreement, the 2030 Agenda, the Sendai Framework). Cities in particular are key actors, given rapid urbanization in Asia and the Pacific. SNGs are crucial for adaptation initiatives and some mitigation efforts. They are estimated to be responsible for 50%–80% of adaptation and mitigation actions. In line with decentralization theory, SNGs can mount an immediate response to disasters and, given accountability and information advantages, can work to protect vulnerable populations and tap into local knowledge for effective planning.

In practice, the potential of SNGs is not being maximized. National policy frameworks on decentralization may be favorable (e.g., the People's Republic of China, Indonesia, and the Philippines) but implementation lags. Attention must be given to clearly assigning climate-related functions to SNGs, with appropriate funding mechanisms. SNGs need authority over sectors relevant to climate change mitigation and adaptation. They must be given the freedom and encouragement to collaborate and engage with international organizations. Climate change action should not be an isolated add-on; it is best integrated into regular SNG planning and budgeting. Ideally, this would be driven by rigorous budget tagging. This is being introduced in some countries in Asia and the Pacific (e.g., India, Nepal, and the Philippines), but definition and data challenges make it difficult to track climate-related expenditures. Tracking expenditure is critical to coherent climate action across government levels. Toward this end, national plans should be disaggregated to show local impacts and encourage complementary SNG efforts. Effective institutional arrangements are also needed for vertical coherence and horizontal alignment within SNGs.

SNGs in Asia and the Pacific face constraints in raising their own revenues for development, including for climate change action. Some countries have low national revenues across all levels of government, hampering SNGs in collecting sufficient revenue to address local climate change challenges—even where citizens sometimes show evidence that they are paying for such services directly, albeit inefficiently. In countries where SNGs have inadequate access to local revenues, intergovernmental fiscal transfers constitute the largest portion of SNG budgets. Some countries are exploring or implementing climate-oriented intergovernmental transfers (ecological fiscal transfers), but these are in the early stages of development (e.g., Indonesia and Viet Nam).

Infrastructure needs in developing Asia and the Pacific are estimated at $26 trillion. Even with public sector financing of climate change action growing nearly 10% annually (2011–2020), SNGs struggle to obtain sufficient funds. Moreover, the financing is fragmented across national funds, and multilateral and bilateral institutions. Despite recognition of SNG importance, allocation remains skewed toward national governments. However, special purpose national climate funds are emerging as a potential channel for SNGs. Additionally, global climate funds (e.g., the Adaptation Fund, the Climate Investment Funds, the Global Environment Facility, the Green Climate Fund) are adding resources to climate change governance. Unfortunately, SNG access to these funds is limited, and often indirect, through national entities or multilateral development banks (MDBs) that generally channel funds through national agencies. "National designated authorities" endorsed by global funds and national funds may not adequately represent SNG perspectives. Less than 10% of global climate finance is dedicated to local actions (2003–2016). Some innovative initiatives linking global funds to SNGs can be seen (e.g., the United Nations Capital Development Fund Local Climate Adaptive Living Facility provides climate-resilient grants to several countries in Asia and the Pacific) and these are particularly useful when they combine finance with capacity building for SNGs. Transnational networks like ICLEI – Local Governments for Sustainability's Transformative Actions Program and C40's Cities Finance Facility also address SNG financing and capacity gaps. The United Cities and Local Government advocates for SNG inclusion in decision-making processes and the strengthening of local finance.

In addressing SNG capacity in climate change governance, the importance of proactive communities through strong SNG leadership becomes evident. Climate change action requires negotiating difficult choices and long-term thinking. Regional and local leaders need to balance short-term needs with sustainability goals. Effective leaders must have skills in communication, trust building, and risk taking. Leaders should inspire citizens and lead by example, as shown in the case of Odanthurai village in India. If climate change investment is to increase, SNG capacities become critical for achieving scale and quality. As indicated earlier, SNGs need support in claiming their roles in climate change action that flow from evolving intergovernmental relationships. An opportunity to build capacity and vertical coherence is the involvement of SNGs in national government-led efforts to develop or revise NDCs and National Adaptation Plans. This is rarely done currently. More broadly, capacity building for SNGs should focus on their ability to plan, coordinate, and finance climate change actions. Support should address approaches to organizing and retaining capable staff for climate-related roles. Thus far, capacity-building efforts have been episodic and poorly designed. There is a lack of comprehensive monitoring and review frameworks to guide long-term capacity building.

SNGs should also be prepared to contribute to performance assessment, helping them improve performance and make their case in securing resources. This is challenging, as weaknesses may persist in defining adaptation initiatives, attributing outcomes, and generating data work against performance assessment. Monitoring, evaluation, and learning systems should be locally appropriate and context-specific.

Enhancing SNG capacity in climate change governance will require substantial support from their respective national governments and development partners. This effort must be aligned within the broader initiative to empower SNGs.

Proper fiscal decentralization is key to maximizing SNG roles in climate change governance. The following recommendations aim to enhance the role of Asia and the Pacific SNGs in climate change governance by addressing key challenges in finance, capacity, and coordination across government levels:

1. Support and expand ongoing efforts, including:
   - standardizing greenhouse gas inventory methodologies at subnational levels;
   - expanding climate risk and vulnerability assessments;
   - integrating climate change actions (including disaster risk reduction and management actions) into planning and budgeting of SNGs;
   - fostering partnerships and inter-SNG cooperation; and
   - creating dedicated climate change units within local administrations.

2. Improve SNG expenditure data collection and analysis:
   - establish an Asia and the Pacific finance hub for SNGs;
   - standardize budget tagging approaches; and
   - analyze climate change funding distribution across countries, SNGs, and population groups.

3. Encourage SNG participation in national climate change policies and plans:
   - establish multistakeholder forums with meaningful SNG involvement;
   - work closely with national SNG associations; and
   - encourage SNGs to prepare scale-appropriate policies/plans.

4. Intensify support for fiscal decentralization:
   - establish clear roles and responsibilities across government levels;
   - develop regular coordination mechanisms;
   - integrate climate change action planning and budgeting across government levels; and
   - boost local taxes and bond issuing for climate change action.

5. Improve SNG access to funds from MDBs and national/global sources:
   - work closer with national SNG associations;
   - form partnerships with global/transnational SNG networks; and
   - facilitate intermediary-level SNGs becoming fund managers.

6. Invest in policy research, evaluation, and knowledge dissemination:
   - focus on both urban and rural contexts; and
   - establish knowledge partnerships for rigorous analysis and lesson sharing.

I. Introduction

This report takes stock of climate change governance at the subnational level in Asia and the Pacific, noting key initiatives, challenges, and enabling factors. It encompasses efforts related to mitigation (reducing carbon dioxide emissions and achieving decarbonization) and adaptation to baked-in impacts of past action and inaction. Subnational governments are varied in their scale, roles, and resources, but as a group they are increasingly acknowledged as important actors in climate governance. This is particularly the case for city governments—the focus of much research[1] and support from development partners.[2] Smaller and rural governments have yet to build a similar profile but are also becoming increasingly proactive. Subnational government (SNG) success in climate change actions,[3] particularly in institutional approaches (governance), is enabled by many factors, with salient ones captured under the rubric of multilevel governance; the linkages between levels of government are critical to fashioning a coherent response to the climate change challenges of both local and national scale. At the national level, these linkages are well captured by the components of fiscal decentralization that describe intergovernmental arrangements that seek to empower SNGs in discharging their roles and functions and in achieving important national goals. In addition, there are important linkages between SNGs and international/global institutions and networks that can add resources and facilitation to the local efforts of SNGs. While data on these initiatives and relationships are still scarce, it is worthwhile to take stock of what is readily discernible to determine the directions being taken and the support most needed at this stage.

This stocktaking report is a desk study that scans the literature pertinent to the Asia and the Pacific and other countries where some comparison is warranted, principally Organisation for Economic Co-operation and Development (OECD) countries where climate change action has been better tracked and assessed. Within Asia and the Pacific, the report draws considerably on the experiences of the Asian Development Bank (ADB), an institution that has provided financing and technical support to various aspects of multilevel governance in its developing member countries—fiscal decentralization, climate change assessments, and climate change-resilient infrastructure being salient. Some of the illustrations are drawn from ADB's financing and technical assistance. ADB funded this study[4] to discover how SNGs can best be supported in undertaking climate change governance in Asia and the Pacific with its interventions and those of other stakeholders.

1 Betsill and Bulkeley (2006); Bulkeley (2010).

2 World Wildlife Fund (2020); ICLEI (2021).

3 Climate change at the subnational government level is closely linked to disaster risk reduction and management, so the discussion on climate change action in the report includes relevant actions in this domain too.

4 Funding was provided by the ADB regional technical assistance 10125: Operationalizing the Community Resilience Partnership Program.

Chapter II briefly outlines the climate change challenges faced by countries in Asia and the Pacific, linking the climate action agenda to the Sustainable Development Goals (SDGs) and the Sendai Framework—global commitments widely supported by nations. The national response to these global frameworks/agreements is covered as a backdrop to the discussion focused on SNGs. Increasingly, climate change action is being grounded within national and local development planning and budgeting processes, but this is done with linkages to many other stakeholders, giving rise to a complex form of multilevel governance. The chapter outlines the architecture of SNGs found in the Asia and the Pacific region and ends by underscoring the potential that SNGs have to contribute to climate change action.

Chapter III breaks down the multilevel governance approach that links national governments to SNGs, employing adapted categories of fiscal decentralization (functional assignment, planning and budgeting, local revenues and borrowing, and intergovernmental grants), noting how climate change action is both enabled and hindered by specific institutional arrangements and resources made available to SNGs.

Chapter IV examines how SNGs can access resources, focusing on financing. The support available from transnational entities (particularly in technical assistance) is also noted, revealing that SNGs in the Asia and the Pacific struggle to obtain direct support. Chapter V addresses the capacity issue that holds SNGs back in addressing climate change, raising the issue of local leadership and ways of bolstering SNG capacity to address climate change in general. The potential role of SNGs in shaping National Determined Contributions (NDCs) and the National Adaptation Plans (NAPs) is recognized. Attention is also given to how SNG performance can be assessed, noting challenges faced in definitions and data availability. In Chapter VI, conclusions are drawn regarding SNG climate change governance and the prospects for greater success. Recommendations are directed to several stakeholders (including ADB).

II. The Climate Change Challenge

A. Climate Change and National Responses in Asia and the Pacific

Climate change is an urgent global challenge threatening ecological sustenance, economic growth, and human development. Higher temperatures, changes in precipitation patterns, glacial melts, extreme events, and sea level rise are impacting the lives and livelihoods of millions across the globe. The impact is skewed toward vulnerable locations and populations. People in highly vulnerable areas are up to 15 times more likely to die in floods, droughts, and storms compared with those in most resilient areas (United Nations 2023). In cities, observed adverse impacts are concentrated among economically and socially marginalized urban residents (IPCC 2023).

The threat posed to Asia and the Pacific is significant, given that it contains the world's largest population as well as 13 of the 30 countries most vulnerable to the impacts of climate change. Densely populated countries like Bangladesh and India contain many of the poorest populations worldwide. In the Pacific, low-lying island nations and coastal areas add to the climate change risk. A high reliance on climate-sensitive sectors like agriculture and fishing compounds this risk. Economic constraints limit many countries' adaptation efforts. With its diverse geography, Asia and the Pacific has witnessed both slow-onset and extreme weather events, with climate change driving the duration and frequency of these. Rising temperatures have increased the likelihood of heatwaves across Asia; droughts in arid and semiarid parts of West, Central, and South Asia; and delays and weakening of the monsoon circulation in South Asia (Shaw, Luo, and Sung 2022). Asia and the Pacific has accounted for 42.4% of global greenhouse gas (GHG) emissions, with 11 high emitters in the region being responsible for 40.8% of global emissions (Economic and Social Commission for Asia and the Pacific [ESCAP] 2021).

Across the region, national commitments to the United Nations Framework Convention on Climate Change (UNFCCC),[5] the Kyoto Protocol, and the Paris Agreement have encouraged policy development and target setting at the country level, particularly in relation to mitigation and transparency of climate action and support. Many countries have enhanced energy efficiency, reduced rates of deforestation, and accelerated technology deployment, thus avoiding emissions and in some cases curtailing these. Most countries have agreed to submit their climate commitments in the form of plans for climate action known as NDCs,[6] spelling out targets, policies, and measures for reducing national emissions. Additionally, NAPs help identify adaptation goals and translate them into action. These rolling NDCs represent "institutionalized, ratified and binding forward-looking commitments" (Dzebo et al. 2019), with an opportunity every 5 years to review country progress toward achieving

[5] The UNFCCC is the United Nations process for negotiating an agreement to limit dangerous climate change.

[6] Nationally determined contributions represent the efforts each country is making to reduce national emissions and adapt to the impacts of climate change. NDCs are submitted every 5 years to the UNFCCC Secretariat.

the commitments. These commitments are complementary to those embodied in the SDGs and the Sendai Framework, which seeks to shift the focus from disaster management to understanding risk and building resilience.

All countries of Asia and the Pacific have submitted their NDCs to the UNFCCC. Some have also prepared the NAPs that flow from the NDCs (Appendix). However, the NDCs fall short of the required climate ambition to effectively reduce GHG emissions to keep the global temperature rise below 1.5°C. The GHG emissions proposed in the NDCs amount to a 16% growth from 2010 emission levels as compared with the 45% reduction in GHG emissions that is required for the region to commit itself to the 1.5°C pathway (ESCAP 2022). While 39 countries of the region have made carbon neutrality[7] pledges (Table 1), some of these are not supported by updated NDC commitments or implementation plans.

The Intergovernmental Panel on Climate Change (IPCC), the United Nations body for assessing the science related to climate change, urges countries to adopt a climate-resilient development pathway that integrates measures to adapt to climate change with actions to reduce emissions in ways that provide wider benefits: improving people's health and livelihoods; reducing poverty and hunger; and providing clean energy, water, and air (IPCC 2023). In this broader development context, national governments must embed climate change policies and programs within their regular planning system,

Table 1: Status of Carbon Neutrality Pledges Across Asia and the Pacific, 2022

Achieved	Adopted Law	Policy Document	Declaration/Pledge	Not Yet Considered
Bhutan	Fiji	Australia	Afghanistan	Bangladesh
	Japan	Cambodia	Brunei Darussalam	Republic of Korea
	Maldives	China, People's Republic of	India	Philippines
	New Zealand	Indonesia	Kiribati	Mongolia
		Kazakhstan	Federated States of Micronesia	Timor-Leste
		Lao People's Democratic Republic	Myanmar	Turkmenistan
		Malaysia	Pakistan	
		Marshall Islands	Palau	
		Nauru	Papua New Guinea	
		Nepal	Samoa	
		Singapore	Tonga	
		Solomon Islands	Tuvalu	
		Sri Lanka	Vanuatu	
		Thailand		
		Viet Nam		

Source: Economic and Social Commission for Asia and the Pacific. 2021. *Asia-Pacific Disaster Report 2021.*

[7] Carbon neutrality is a state of net-zero CO_2 emissions.

putting into play the bulk of their resources rather than treating climate change action merely as one of the many and standalone claims on the national budget. These embedded policies and programs will naturally implicate other stakeholders, particularly the private sector, civil society, and SNGs that are already committed to the development effort. Their combined interactions give rise to institutions, resources, and practices that can be labeled "climate change governance."

Finally, national governments should be able to count on global solidarity efforts to accelerate their efforts to address climate change. The financial and technical resources available to national governments and SNGs are increasing, and mechanisms have been put in place to allow national entities to shape interventions and their implementation (Chapter IV). However, tapping these resources is unduly difficult for SNGs. Allocating these resources equitably and effectively to empower SNGs to play their part fully in addressing climate change is a challenge that has not been squarely met and will need to be approached with a greater appreciation for how these resources fit within or alongside the diverse intergovernmental institutional arrangements that characterize fiscal decentralization in countries across Asia and the Pacific.

B. Conceptual Framework for Subnational Government Climate Change Governance

Awareness of the impact of human activities in the release of GHGs into the atmosphere is a starting point for government and stakeholder action. Recognizing that it is necessary, and feasible, to avert the impending disaster that runaway climate change can bring is key to shaping motivations and action. While countries and specific populations are at different stages in appreciating these realities, consensus is growing that climate change action is needed on many fronts, through activities, mechanisms, and policies that can reduce the severity of human-induced climate change and its impacts. This growing consensus is essential in generating "demand" for mitigation and adaptation measures.

Doing something about climate change requires acknowledging its impacts in terms of their scale and downstream effects over time. The impact may originate in a given region, but it spreads over time to affect other regions. This has been recognized at a global level (Carter et al. 2021) but needs to be underscored as a dynamic also applicable within countries, thereby implicating neighboring communities and regions in the same national space in climate change action. Policies and planning may well be generated by political/administrative bodies with defined boundaries, but these bodies need to think and act in terms of the functional or impact areas that result from climate change. Climate change action necessarily entails a range of settings and specific approaches, implicating different territorial scales, sectors, and actors who must find ways of addressing issues within their locality and across jurisdictions. As Figure 1 shows, mitigation and adaptation actions are situated within a set of relationships, tools, or methods. These include technology, finance, and approaches to test whether interventions work. Many actors can become involved in these efforts, in a leading or supportive role. New institutions are sometimes established, combining sets of actors or existing organizations. These actors/organizations sometimes combine as temporary or permanent networks. The institutional arrangements put in place to counter climate change impact are subsumed under the rubric of climate change governance (hence they are not limited to government) precisely because they can encompass this broad swath of actors, coordinating or collaborating in many ways. This collaboration has of course culminated in global conventions like the UNFCCC and the Paris Agreement, and these in turn provide a framework for national commitments that necessarily implicate all of the country-level actors in multilevel governance, as Figure 1 shows.

Figure 1 shows that the institutional ecosystem for climate change at national level is very complex. Governments must work closely with many stakeholders to shape and implement policies. They do this also with reference to the agreements and the influence of global actors concerned with climate change issues (e.g., the SDG framework of the United Nations, or financing opportunities from organizations like ADB). Government itself must be unbundled to discern the roles of discrete levels of government, noting the degree of decentralization, particularly for functions closely related to climate change action. A useful way of further dissecting government in the context of decentralization is to examine key elements of fiscal decentralization/financial management, as adapted from Smoke (2001) and Martinez-Vazquez (2021) among others:

1. functional assignment (who does what);
2. planning and budgeting systems;
3. revenue assignment and borrowing; and
4. intergovernmental grants.

Figure 1: Conceptual Framework for Climate Change and Its Multilevel Governance Context

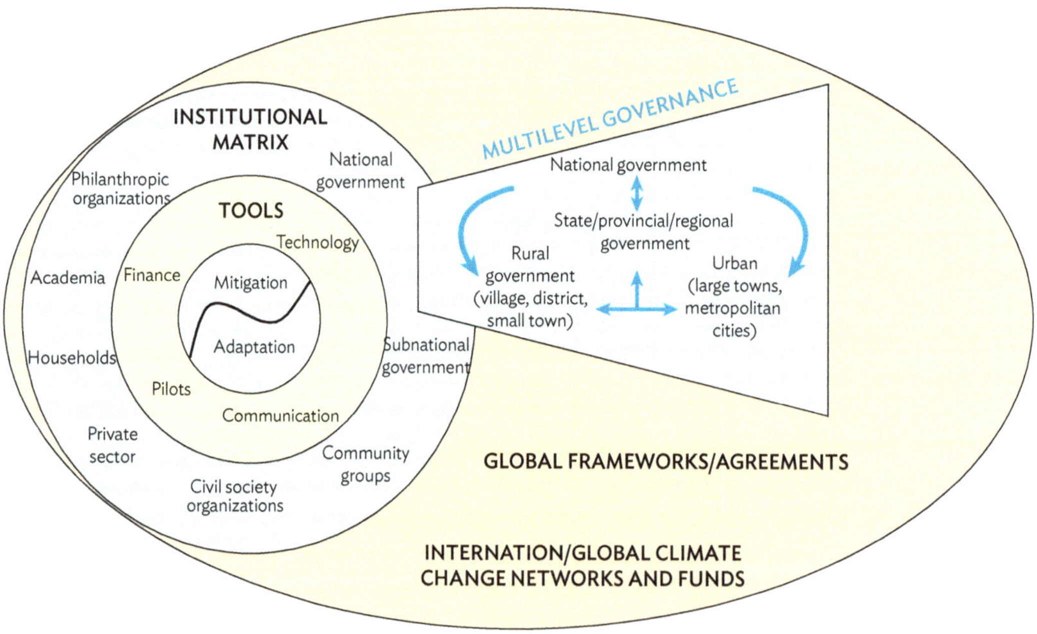

Source: Author.

Functional assignment determines the scope of activities of SNGs, and whether creativity and initiative are encouraged. Narrowly crafted positive lists (beyond which action becomes ultra-vires—i.e., beyond the strict confines of enumerated lists found in the legal framework) can constrain SNGs, rendering their political autonomy less meaningful. General competence (e.g., Home Rule in the United States) can give SNGs the lead role and room for local initiative with permissive formulations of what they can undertake; this approach allows SNGs to act on their perceptions of need and opportunities, rather than strictly follow an explicit menu. A general competence (or other explicit right of initiative) also allows SNGs to be creative in pursuing their objectives, establishing new structures and partnerships with other SNGs and nongovernment partners. Hybrid forms, often purposeful or the result of tinkering, can bring some functions into relief (as those that must be undertaken—i.e., are obligatory) while still allowing for local initiative, provided there is no obvious encroachment on assigned functions of higher levels of government (Ferrazzi and Rohdewohld 2017). As climate change action cuts across many sectors/services, the formal functional assignment architecture and weight of functions assigned can make SNGs important actors in mitigation and adaptation efforts. A limited and rigidly defined set of functions can instead stifle SNG efforts. Countries in Asia and the Pacific exhibit a wide range of decentralization in this regard, with the People's Republic of China (PRC), Indonesia, and the Philippines being examples of countries with empowered SNGs. Countries like Cambodia, Maldives, and Myanmar—despite some attempts at decentralization—remain heavily centralized.

Planning and budgeting systems are key to translating assigned functions into concrete programs, and these processes are where functions and interests across levels of government can be made explicit and lead to coordinated spending for maximum effect in pursuing national targets. The key is to share sufficient information and guidance while avoiding transaction-heavy mechanisms of coordination. Coherent and dovetailing policies, and respect for assigned functions in planning processes, should generate synergy across levels of government and help avoid duplication of effort or working at cross-purposes. For instance, conservation efforts of SNGs need to be linked to national road-building policies to limit access.

SNGs need adequate resources to undertake their assigned functions, and several options are used to achieve this objective. Raising substantial own revenues is widely encouraged in the fiscal decentralization literature, to ensure accountability to local taxpayers, and to increase the fiscal capacity of SNGs to undertake their mandates without having to rely on central governments. In many countries, this will not be sufficient to cover all SNG expenditures, and the capacity to raise revenues from local taxes and charges is highly variable across same-tier SNGs. For instance, metropolitan centers in Asia can raise substantial proportions of the revenue needed to discharge their functions, but wide differences in fiscal capacity are nonetheless evident, arising in large part from the willingness of national government to allow property taxation, and for cities to make use of this source (Bahl 2018). Fiscal capacity can be enhanced through borrowing (from banks or issuing bonds), but capital market access and good debt management are required of SNGs in this case (Bahl and Martinez-Vasquez 2022). Financial intermediation programs operated by national governments can facilitate borrowing but such programs are vulnerable to political capture and low repayment rates.

Intergovernmental grants are designed to close the vertical fiscal gap arising from the functions assigned to SNGs as compared with the local revenue sources made available. They also can equalize widely varying fiscal capacities of SNGs (horizontal equalization). An objective formula-based set of grants is an important component of a stable, equitable, and efficient system of intergovernmental fiscal relations (Boex and Martinez-Vasquez 2005). In practice, political considerations find their way into the allocations. Competitive or bottom-up proposal-based approaches can in principle cater to specific needs, but heavy transaction costs and bias toward the more capable and politically connected SNGs can reduce the equalization effect.

Hampering the application of the fiscal decentralization framework is the difficulty faced in measuring climate-related expenditures—of national governments or SNGs. The latter often are responsible for some environmental services (e.g., parks/conservation, waste management) but SNGs also spend on forests/agriculture management, public transportation, renewable energy projects, and many more items that could potentially have a bearing on climate change mitigation or adaptation. How to count all of these to determine expenditure on climate change action is challenging, as is doing so consistently across SNG and countries.

The information gap also makes it difficult for development partners to discern where the gaps between need and fiscal capacity are greatest. Even so, a notable source of climate change financing and technical support for SNGs is global funds, networks, and other actors (e.g., SNG associations, philanthropic organizations). While these have been directed mostly to national governments, they potentially could reach SNG directly or through nationally conditioned mechanisms.

C. Subnational Government Structures and Potential Roles in Asia and the Pacific

The government actors listed in Figure 1 include the national level and SNGs. Many countries in Asia and the Pacific, by virtue of their size, have more than one subnational level of government (e.g., India has five) and even the smaller countries can have multiple SNG levels (e.g., Cambodia with three). The distinction between regional/intermediate and local government can sometimes be blurry, and some countries have unique administrative structures that do not perfectly fit this two-column format. Nomenclature is not always indicative of scale if compared across countries. For instance, the district is a lower-level government in Indonesia but may have a larger population[8] than the provincial-level government or of some Pacific small island countries.

Countries in Asia and the Pacific also differ in terms of the basic state structure, with knock-on effects on institutional arrangements and relationships between levels of government. Most are unitary states (e.g., the PRC, Indonesia, and the Philippines, and most island states in the Pacific), where the national-level state institutions (particularly the executive) are dominant,[9] and SNGs tends to be considerably constrained in their autonomy. A few are federal in structure (e.g., India, Malaysia, Nepal, and Pakistan), potentially giving the formative units (e.g., states, regions, and provinces) more autonomy politically, functionally, and in generating resources. This distinction should not be held rigidly; unitary states like the PRC and Indonesia are more decentralized than some federal states (like Malaysia and Nepal). It is also worth noting that some unitary states will emphasize

8 For instance, Bandung district at 3.7 million is more populous than the province of Papua, or of the entire nation of Solomon Islands.

9 In this report, the state is understood to be the complex of institutions that governs a country, often comprising a division of power across the primary branches—legislative, executive, and judicial. Government is understood as the executive branch (if strictly defined), but more loosely used can imply the executive together with the legislative.

decentralization (at least initially) for lower levels of government rather than the larger subnational governments (e.g., Cambodia's communes over its districts, Indonesia's districts over its provinces). These differences call for an appreciation of the country context to understand the scope of SNG climate change governance and how multilevel governance unfolds.

Figure 1 cannot capture the full richness of multilevel governance. In simplified form, it outlines the government hierarchy in the expanded wing, showing a typical government architecture of the majority of governments around the world. These government hierarchies are necessarily embedded within the larger society, connected through elections and other participatory mechanisms. In some nations in the region, there may be additional layers of government; some urban centers may have a privileged direct link to the national government rather than through a regional level. In some countries, the national reach to the lowest levels of government is limited (especially in federal states), whereas in others it can be considerable, making the guidance of these lower levels a complex interaction. This is seen in Bangladesh, Indonesia, and the Philippines.

This reach (or intrusion) of the national government in SNG governance can have a salutary or undermining effect on multilevel governance. If properly employed, it can reinforce a form of multilevel governance that gives more options in attracting resources and support to otherwise small or isolated rural SNGs. It can encourage and channel local needs and aspirations in bottom-up processes, giving them consideration in higher-level planning events (e.g., medium-term planning or annual coordination). Moreover, national involvement and influence over SNGs can generate vertical coherence from national level down through the regional SNG to the city/rural SNG, melding local action with national priorities and resources; the regional level (intermediary level) in this case plays a strategic linking role. The downside of such national reach can be an insufficient and sporadic kind of support to the lower-level SNG if the regional level is bypassed. National directives may propagate standard solutions that do not fit with regional/local contexts. Messages from the national and regional level may not be consistent, and the mediating and bridging potential of the regional-level SNG is underutilized. Table 2 shows the possible and complementary roles to be played by the various levels of government (Corfee-Morlot et al. 2009). If some of these roles are prohibited for certain SNGs, or not made feasible, the potential of the SNG in addressing climate change is correspondingly reduced.

Table 2: Climate Change and Multilevel Governance—Indicative Framework of Key Actors and Roles at Different Scales of Action

Key Actors and Roles	National	Large Subnational Government (e.g., States, Regions, Provinces)	Small Subnational Government (Rural, Towns, Small Cities)
Government roles	• National commitments to global treaties: nationally determined contributions, national adaptation plans • National laws and policies (e.g., energy, air pollution, water)	• Implementation of national laws, standards • Laws and policies in key climate-related sectors (e.g., energy, air pollution, water) • Sectoral planning and objective setting	• Implementing local decisions as foreseen under national or subnational law • Decision-making on delegated/devolved functions relating to climate actions (water conservation, management, waste management, etc.)

continued on next page

Table 2 *continued*

Key Actors and Roles	National	Large Subnational Government (e.g., States, Regions, Provinces)	Small Subnational Government (Rural, Towns, Small Cities)
	• Sectoral planning and objective setting • Standards and performance regulation • Oversight and coordination across sectors • Fiscal provisioning, incentivization • Infrastructure funding and provisioning • Establishing and managing a national inventory system • Enabling technology and knowledge acquisition • Identifying, leading, supporting transnational cooperation on climate problems with externalities (river flooding, silting, etc.) • Organizing meteorological data • Capacity development frameworks and resources • Vulnerability assessments and disaster risk characterization, preparedness, response, and recovery codes and protocols at national scale • Monitoring policies and actions • Knowledge and data provisioning for subnational and local decision-making on climate issues • Representing national actions and challenges in global forums	• Ensuring vertical and horizontal coordination • Standards and performance regulation permitted by national laws • Oversight and coordination across sectors • Reporting on national monitoring indicators • Fiscal provisioning, incentivization • Infrastructure funding and provisioning • Prioritization and time frame setting for regional action (e.g., by sector) • Providing incentives, funding, and authorization to enable local action on climate change • Vulnerability assessments and disaster risk preparedness and response systems • Monitoring systems • Guiding, supporting, enabling, funding, regulating local actions • Capacity building of state and non-state stakeholders • Membership of international networks	• Enabling vertical and horizontal coordination • Ensuring convergence across sectoral plans and actions • Reporting on national and subnational monitoring functions • Supporting and showcasing innovations for upscaling • Identifying local priorities: enhancing local/regional understanding, working with local actors • Raising awareness • Advocating, where needed, for locally adapted policies and measures • Capacity building of state and non-state stakeholders • Supporting local actions
Key institutions or actors	• National ministries/ departments • Autonomous institutions (pollution control boards, fiscal commissions) • Semiautonomous public institutions (e.g., training institutions, renewable energy missions, climate change commissions) • Private sector: industry associations • Universities	• State or provincial governmental authorities • Representatives of national authorities • Semiautonomous public (issue-based commissions, boards, training institutions) • Associations (elected representatives, users) • Industries/corporations • Academic institutions	• Public authorities • Representatives of national and subnational authorities • Local industry • User groups

Source: Adapted from J. Corfee-Morlot et al. 2009. *Cities, Climate Change and Multilevel Governance*. Environmental Working Paper. OECD.

D. Potential Contribution of Subnational Governments to Climate Change Governance

Over the past 2 decades, the potential contribution of SNGs in addressing climate change has come to the fore, becoming more visibly embedded in the Paris Agreement and other global and national frameworks. Box 1 captures the link between climate change and related global agendas.

Box 1: Recognition of Subnational and Local Actions in Global Agendas

Paris Agreement
The agreement recognizes in its preamble the significance of engagement of all levels of government to address climate change, specifically highlighting their role regarding adaptation, loss and damage, and capacity building.

Agenda 2030
In pursuing Agenda 2030, governments and public institutions commit to "work closely on implementation with regional and local authorities, subregional institutions, international institutions, academia, philanthropic organizations, volunteer groups and others."

Sendai Framework for Disaster Risk Reduction 2015–2030
The framework stresses the importance of local action in stating "international, regional, subregional and transboundary cooperation remains pivotal in supporting the efforts of States, their national and local authorities, as well as communities and businesses, to reduce disaster risk."

Sources: United Nations Framework Convention on Climate Change. 2015. *The Paris Agreement*; United Nations. 2015a. *Transforming Our World: The 2030 Agenda for Sustainable Development*; United Nations. 2015b. *Sendai Framework for Disaster Risk Reduction 2015–2030*.

Cities are recognized as hotspots for the effects of emissions, loss and damage, vulnerabilities, exposure, and impacts. Asia and the Pacific comprises 60% of the world population and includes fast-urbanizing regions and megacities (UNFPA 2023). Over 50% of the population in this region now lives in cities. Accordingly, cities are seen as being key climate actors (IPCC 2024). Rural SNGs have received less recognition but are particularly concerned about, and active in, adaptation issues. Taken as a whole, SNGs are still on the periphery of global and national policy in some respects. For instance, the NDC Partnership (2020) notes that the development of most NDCs lacks the meaningful involvement of subnational actors.

Key issues raised by SNGs in the NDC Partnership include lack of clear roles and responsibilities between national and subnational levels in implementing NDCs, limited data availability, insufficient fiscal decentralization preventing local governments from implementing large-scale climate projects, and limited local government authority to enforce green building codes and low-carbon urban planning (NDC Partnership 2020). These highlight the important need for strong coordination and collaboration between national and SNG actions. For instance, national transportation policy may allow SNG to regulate some aspects of transportation at the local level (e.g., public transport fares and idling of vehicles). Globally, over 40% of GHG emissions are estimated to emanate from activities over which subnational governments exert some degree of regulatory and taxing authority (Martinez-Vasquez 2021). It is also widely acknowledged that SNGs are well placed to support adaptation initiatives. This is understandable in view of the obvious interest of SNGs and their stakeholders in facing the impacts of climate change that arise in particular form and intensity in their locality; they are on the frontline of climate change action.

Regions4 Sustainable Development, a growing cooperation body for subnational government, estimates that 50%–80% of adaptation and mitigation actions already are or will be implemented at the regional and local levels.[10] Many of the functions that fall in the purview of SNGs, such as water provision, sanitation and drainage, housing, local economic development, public health and emergency management, and ecosystem restoration and management are vulnerable to climate change impacts and provide possibilities to strengthen adaptive capacities to improve climate resilience (OECD 2019a). Smaller/rural SNGs also have the potential to protect poor and vulnerable groups and enable them to better withstand and adapt to climate risks. For instance, their actions can be directed to diversifying household incomes to reduce their vulnerability to climatic stresses. This bottom-up approach to planning and decision-making can tap into local knowledge of risks and ways to adapt. It behooves national governments to strengthen formal and informal institutions at the local/regional level to assist them in managing climate risks and ensure the sustainability of the investments (Mogelgaard et al. 2018).

10 Regions4 Sustainable Development. https://regions4.org/our-work/climate-change/.

III. Enabling Subnational Government Climate Change Action Through Fiscal Decentralization

A. Giving Subnational Governments the Authority to Address Climate Change

In many countries of Asia and the Pacific, the need to involve SNGs in climate governance is well recognized but has yet to be sufficiently translated into meaningful policies, legal frameworks, and programming. As noted in the case of Cambodia, the "mainstreaming" of climate change at subnational level that appears in policy documents and strategic plans has been slow in practice (Ministry of Environment and UNDP 2011, World Bank 2024). The lagging step in Cambodia, as in several other countries desiring a stronger SNG role in climate governance, is the formal assignment of functions in governmental matters/functions that are critical to fighting climate change. This formal assignment is a prerequisite for crafting consistent institutional arrangements on SNG staffing and intergovernmental finances (Ferrazzi and Rohdewohld 2017). In the case of Cambodia, the very elaborate policies on the district and village level and protracted processes for determining which functions SNAs (subnational administrations in Cambodian terminology) should be given have only recently resulted in some significant functions (e.g., rural development and waste management) that can give SNAs meaningful levels of control over climate change action. Box 2 shows how Cambodia has done well on policy but could do more to follow through with specific measures to empower SNAs to act on climate change.

A second shortcoming in most countries relates to missteps in assigning functions to SNGs without properly deciding whether these are obligatory (mandatory) or optional (voluntary/discretionary/permissive). Obligatory functions are generally those that affect citizens daily and are essential to their survival and wellbeing—mostly basic services such as health and education. Usually, these have performance expectations tied to them and are funded largely through conditional transfers from the national government. Optional functions are instead generally left to SNGs to conceive and implement, in accordance with their felt needs and resources. Climate change-related actions tend not to be well conceived and standardized in terms of governmental functions or budget codes—because they have emerged more recently and because they are often cross-sector in nature. Governments that on paper commit to climate change and decentralization are often nonetheless hesitant to assign to SNGs clear and weighty functions on a service/sector basis (those connected

Box 2: Cambodia—Strong Policies but Slow Follow-Through on Functions and Resources for Subnational Administrations to Fight Climate Change

In 2013, the Government of Cambodia approved the Cambodia Climate Change Strategic Plan 2014–2023 as an overarching national framework to respond to climate change. It formulates a vision for Cambodia to develop toward a green, low-carbon, climate-resilient, equitable, sustainable, and knowledge-based society. So far, 14 line ministries have developed sector climate change strategic plans and sector climate change action plans to operationalize them, and more are expected to do so since the Ministry of Planning issued guidelines for mainstreaming climate change in the 2019–2023 cycle.

While in principle the Cambodia Climate Change Strategic Plan is aligned with the deconcentration and decentralization reform of the country (which also goes back more than a decade), it has not yet led to widespread mainstreaming of climate change into subnational administration (SNA) plans and budgets. The November 2014 Climate Change Financing Framework sought to achieve a common approach but lacked useful guidelines and tools to mobilize and manage financial resources for climate change, especially for SNAs. Domestic sources (the national budget) accounted for 29% of expenditures in climate change, while external sources (development partners) covered 71%.

According to the National Committee for Subnational Democratic Development Secretariat, around 60 of the 185 districts of the country (32% of them) have done some climate change planning, although not all communes in each of these districts have been covered. The main contributors to implementing these local plans have been development partners rather than government funds. The data does not show a consistent increase in the funds spent by SNAs on climate change response in recent years.

As these findings indicate, climate public expenditure has concentrated on the central government. Climate change expenditure by ministries represented 97% of total climate change expenditure in the 2012–2017 period, and the trend is toward greater centralization in spending. Climate change expenditure of SNAs and nongovernment organizations has been limited: it represented 1% and 1.9%, respectively, in that period. This pattern coexists with the above-mentioned well-elaborated national policy framework and a long-standing deconcentration and decentralization reform that was to empower the communes and district governments (the more numerous and rural SNAs in Cambodia). What is not noted in recent evaluations of climate change is that the latter reforms have yet to be concluded, and most of the functions related to climate change are still in the hands of the central government. Decentralization has been felt largely in the education sector.[a] Some movement has recently been noted in rural development and solid waste management. This lag between policy and the legal functional assignment (that will also require attendant resources) goes a long way in explaining the very incomplete, episodic, and externally funded nature of climate change action in rural SNAs in Cambodia.

[a] National Committee for Subnational Democratic Development. 2023. Report on Results of the Evaluation of the Management, Administration and Implementation of Educational Function Transferred to the Municipal & District/Khan Administration. Supported by NCDDS and ISD/GIZ Programs.

Source: National Council for Sustainable Development (Cambodia). 2019. Mid-Term Review of Cambodia Climate Change Strategic Plan 2014 – 2023. Final Evaluation Report. Supported by CCCA and UNDP.

with large budgets or revenues), given the loss in roles, status, and resources this entails for them.[11] They will sometimes simply leave the functional assignment unclear to avoid commitment or urge SNGs to take the initiative using "optional" functions. These are generally underfunded or not funded at all by the national government.

Cities can sometimes make progress despite an ambiguous legal framework by virtue of their substantial own revenue sources. Unless they are stopped by higher-level government, they proceed with locally designed actions that match their financial capacity. Smaller/rural SNGs often do not have such resources and thus do not take advantage of the implied right to take the initiative or higher-level government tolerance of local action that is not strictly coded (e.g., part of an enumerated list of assigned functions). They must rely more on higher-level transfers that are usually earmarked, reducing their ability to identify climate change threats and to act on them on their own initiative.

Another misstep in functional assignment is allowing too much concurrence.[12] When done carefully and purposefully, concurrence can enjoin multiple levels to engage and collaborate on broad challenges like climate change. However, when concurrence is simply a way of avoiding hard decisions on which level should be taking the lead or have exclusive domain, then the architecture can result in tension between levels, duplication, or gaps in action as a consequence of a lack of ownership of any one level. Box 3 on Nepal shows how excessive concurrence can be; several of the concurrent functions relate closely to climate change.

Box 3: Concurrent Powers of Federal, Provincial, and Local Governments

The following are areas of governance with authority shared by federal, provincial, and local governments:

- Cooperatives;
- Education, health, and newspapers/magazines;
- Health;
- Agriculture;
- Services like electricity, drinking water, and irrigation;
- Service fees, registration fees, fines, tourism fees, and royalties received from natural resources;
- Forest, wildlife, birds, water use, environment, ecology, and biodiversity;
- Mines and minerals;
- Disaster management;
- Social security and poverty alleviation;
- Registration of personal incidents, births, deaths, marriages, and statistics;
- Archaeology, ancient monuments, and museums;
- Management of landlessness; and
- Royalties received from natural resources

Source: Schedule 9 of the 2015 Constitution of Nepal.

11 The losses felt by national-level actors may be real (e.g., funds shifted from ministries to intergovernmental grants—which can also mean losing control over legitimate and illegal sources of personal income) or psychological (e.g., having reduced staff numbers or not being greeted with the same enthusiasm when visiting the regions).

12 Concurrence in this context means where the very same functions are assigned to two or more levels of government, or when the formulation is distinguished only by adding "at the scale of the...," which often does not help at all in discerning differences in what is applicable or undertaken.

Even with a favorable assignment of functions, it is important to note whether these functions now in the hands of SNGs will be taken up by elected officials or officials appointed by higher-level government. Elected officials are more likely to push for innovation and a local perspective than an appointed SNG leadership. In either case, cities, especially large cities, will likely have more political heft and autonomy, even when the mayor/governor is appointed. This relative autonomy can also be found in some regional SNGs endowed with a thriving economic base. Smaller rural SNGs with appointed leaders (as in Kazakhstan and Uzbekistan) tend to toe the official line and are thus largely implementors of top-down programs; they will rarely have the resources, or the desire, to take risks in advancing their own initiatives. The case of Uzbekistan (Box 4) shows how SNGs can be constrained in fighting climate change by scale, architecture, and functions.

Linking the lower-level governments to their higher-level government is an obvious answer to the challenges noted in Uzbekistan. This can be hardwired into the functional assignment architecture, particularly in unitary states, where both national and regional governments can be given a guidance role over lower levels of government. This dual guidance can allow SNGs to lean on two levels of higher-level government. However, if the central/federal level unduly intrudes on lower-level SNG matters, it may undermine the "intermediary" role of the regional level. This has been noted in Indonesia, for example, where the provincial level has historically been kept in check in favor of central government direct engagement with district and village governments. This has made the support for these levels insufficient, episodic, and rather incoherent as the messages between central and regional government may not mesh. Even so, astute rural districts and small cities can skillfully harness both provincial and central support. Box 5 outlines the efforts made in Indonesia to maximize the dual role of the regional government head (governor) in bringing about effective multilevel governance in climate change.

Box 4: Subnational Governments Constrained in Climate Action—the Case of Uzbekistan

Uzbekistan is highly vulnerable to climate change and particularly exposed to water stress; water scarcity and land degradation threaten agricultural productivity and food security. As part of the wave of reforms following the election of a new government in 2017, Uzbekistan is pursuing a green transition that calls for the engagement of local governments and self-governing communities (*mahallas*). In line with this, the president has voiced his commitment to allowing direct election of regional and district/city representatives (*hokims*). Mahallas, meanwhile, have long elected their own leadership. One of their tasks is to convey community needs and aspirations to local officials. However, because of their small scale (2,000–3,000 people) and inward focus, mahallas have tended to simply support centrally directed schemes like afforestation drives. The higher-level governments (*hokimiyats*: provinces and districts) have more resources but are more responsive to the interests and programs of the central government than to the requests and views of mahallas and citizens. The promise of elections of leaders of these levels, announced in 2016, has yet to be made good. Some of their climate-related functions, like water distribution and solid waste management, have recently been recentralized—to involve the private sector in a direct link to the central government. Given the scale (mahallas), orientation, and climate change functions (hokimiyats), SNGs in Uzbekistan are not realizing their full potential in climate change action.

Sources: World Bank. 2022a. *Green Growth and Climate Change in Uzbekistan Policy Dialogue Series: A Compendium of Proceedings;* ADB. 2023. *Uzbekistan: Validation of the Country Partnership Strategy Final Review.*

Box 5: The Dual Role of the Provincial Governor in Climate Governance in Indonesia

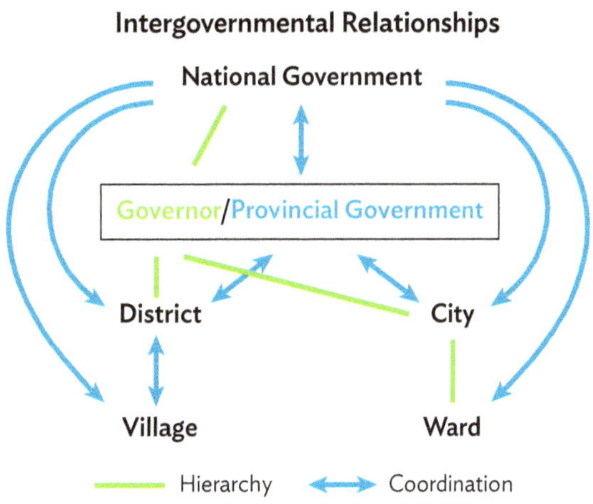

Provincial governors in Indonesia have been asked by the central government to give more attention to understanding climate change and developing policies to deal with it. Governors are to help regional governments (provinces and districts/cities) make the fullest use of their assigned functions in addressing climate change challenges.[a] The governor provides this leadership and supervision in his role as a representative of the central government. They must also ensure provinces and districts carry out an inventory of GHG emissions. An additional task is to encourage district governments to foster local-level activities that are nationally sponsored, particularly the Climate Village Program (ProKlim) initiated in 2012, which has already reached 2,775 villages/wards and is expected to reach 20,000 locations by 2024. The governor is also responsible for forwarding successful village initiatives under ProKlim to the national level to possibly be recognized nationally with awards. More formally, this reporting upward is conducted as part of the governor's supervision function, where regional government efforts and results in pursuing NDC targets are captured in a National Registry System (box figure).

More broadly, the governor leads the preparation of SDG action plans, which include climate change-related goals and targets. They must involve the districts/city governments. They are also responsible for ensuring these SDG action plans are incorporated in the comprehensive development plans of the provincial and district/city governments.

This role of the governor as a representative of the central government dovetails with his or her role as directly elected provincial head, accountable to citizens through the provincial council. As the supervision and support function required by the central government must be funded, the governor can switch roles and enjoin his or her own provincial administration to provide funding from the provincial budget to carry out these tasks. The governor must also work with the provincial council to find resources to enable technical provincial departments to provide support to districts and villages, as the governor does not have any technical central government staff under his or her control. When the governor plays his or her cards well, the benefits of the deconcentration stream (governor as representative of the central government) and decentralized stream (governor as provincial head) generates synergy and a coherent multilevel approach, binding national local levels in a concerted effort.

GHG = greenhouse gas, NDC = nationally determined contribution, SDG = Sustainable Development Goal.
[a] See, for instance, the circular disseminated by the Minister of Environment and Forestry, Siti Nurbaya, dated 19 January 2022, addressed to the governors of provinces throughout Indonesia (Kementerian Lingkungan Hidup dan Kehutanan 2022).
Sources: Partnership in Transparency. 2022. Strengthening Community Level Climate Change Adaptation and Mitigation Actions: Indonesia's Climate Village Programme (ProKlim); and, G. Ferrazzi. *2023. Indonesia's Decentralized Approach to Achieving the Sustainable Development Goals.* In B. Carrasco, H. Rahemtulla, and R. Rohdewohld, eds. Decentralization, Local Governance, and Localizing the Sustainable Development Goals in Asia and the Pacific. ADB/Routledge.

Another way of empowering SNGs is to ensure they have sufficient authority over those sectors or issues that relate to climate change mitigation and adaptation. Given the cross-sector nature of climate change impacts, which tend to not respect jurisdictional boundaries, it is tempting for higher-level government bureaucracies to promote a form of functional assignment that is "functional" in the sense that it escapes territorial government control through the tracing of boundaries that cross SNG territorial/administrative limits.[13] This often makes good sense, as in the example of watersheds, forests, or conservation areas that are distinct ecosystems and need integrated management that follows natural contours. In these cases, it is nonetheless possible and advisable to give SNGs a role, if not the primary role, in managing these areas. For example, all of the implicated SNGs could be placed on the governing bodies of these management entities. They would essentially be co-managing the natural resources, quite likely within a framework shaped by the national level.

SNGs can also be empowered through functional assignment by ensuring they are front and center in engagement with civil society and the private sector and have the authority to accept funds and other resources from them. In this respect, higher-level government would be expected to avoid efforts to retain resources at higher levels and circumvent SNGs, going directly to communities/civil society organizations that are within the SNGs. These centralized approaches to local action tend to have a uniform approach, whereas local communities, if properly supported, tend to focus on the smaller, more frequent disasters and the stresses that confront them. Lower-level SNGs are often best placed to engage these communities to identify and address these disasters and stresses. Favoring locally led adaptation in principle (IIED 2024) would be consistent with the principle of subsidiarity, where the lowest level of government that can effectively carry out a task is entrusted with the task.

A favorable functional assignment also ensures that SNGs have the explicit authority to collaborate with other SNGs domestically and to engage with international organizations. This authority would include an openness to creating various structures of coordination and cooperation, such as joint secretariats or corporate entities to share service delivery. Decentralization reforms in Indonesia have opened opportunities for this form of collaboration, encouraging agreements and new structures to pursue service delivery efforts and allowing SNGs to form local government associations. It also allows the formation of linkages to foreign organizations. Some provinces have forged agreements (with national facilitation) with foreign governments or agencies to address climate change. For instance, Nusa Tenggara Barat province joined with the Danish Energy Agency to accelerate the transition to clean energy (Dinas Energy dan Sumber Daya Mineral 2021).

B. Integrating Climate Change Action in Planning and Budgeting

1. Attaining Vertical and Horizontal Coordination

To the extent that SNGs are given substantial functions across climate change-related sectors, there will be a need to undertake sound planning and budgeting for these functions at the SNG level, as well as vertical planning/coordination to ensure they fit with national plans and budgets.

[13] For a grounding on this territory/function divide, see the early writing of Friedmann and Weaver (1979).

As indicated earlier (on the SNG conceptual framework for climate change action), ideally climate change actions should be integrated within the regular SNG policymaking, planning, and budgeting process. In line with international best practices, policy coherence between national and subnational governments should be established with climate change targets and indicators effectively integrated in the policies and local development plans and projects. Medium-term fiscal frameworks and annual budgeting should incorporate these plans and projects so they are implemented. Further, a monitoring framework should also be coherent (between national and subnational governments) to regularly track implementation progress, to identify issues so mid-course corrections can be made, and to draw lessons for future project design and implementation.

One way to make this more concrete for climate change action is to establish some guidance at the SNG policy level that will provide parameters for the process. This is sometimes done under the banner of a green budget. This can serve as guidance, or at least a reminder, for planners of various levels and sectors to stay focused on certain objectives, like carbon neutrality by 2050. Normally, the national government will set such goals and have metrics for it; in the absence of such guidance, it is up to SNGs to craft their own, based on local considerations and emerging good practices internationally. National governments must have some capability to encourage and guide these SNG planning and budgeting efforts. Recognizing that capacity is weak on all levels for these processes, global networks have come into existence to provide assistance, such as the Under2 Coalition, which seeks to connect state, regional, provincial, and subnational governments from around the world to further its Next Generation Budget and other initiatives (Under2 Coalition 2024). Some support is also provided by multilateral development banks (MDBs). ADB, for instance, is helping Cambodia's national government and SNGs to mainstream climate resilience in development planning (ADB 2022).

The vertical coherence alluded to above is critical to making the most of limited resources in the pursuit of national climate commitments as found in NDC and NAP targets. It begins with policy coherence.[14] National objectives and targets need to percolate downward to influence regional/local government policies. The national government could well impose these in a heavy-handed way to ensure alignment, but then it would forgo the ownership and commitment that a meaningful degree of regional/local autonomy would engender. For this reason, a national and inclusive dialogue is advisable, ideally involving associations of SNGs. The intent would be to converge on the nature/extent of climate change threats; how negative impacts are felt at local level and can spill over SNG boundaries; the importance of climate change actions and incentives that can be provided to SNGs to act; and understanding respective roles and linkages across levels of government given the scale of climate change externalities.[15] SNGs should be encouraged to fashion regional/local climate change action policies that arise from their own conditions and complement those announced at national level. Equally important, the national level should provide opportunities to SNG associations and other stakeholders to shape national policies, recognizing that SNGs are more knowledgeable about local climate impacts and adaptation needs and which solutions are most acceptable. These solutions, imbued with local information and knowledge, in turn need to be informed by scientific knowledge, expertise, and related resources, which are most often found at national level (Carrasco, Rahemtulla, and Rohdewohld 2022).

[14] Policy coherence implies the various policies addressing an area are compatible, mutually reinforcing, and synergistic (Dzebo et al. 2019).

[15] See, for instance, NDC Partnership (2020) and Martinez-Vazquez (2021).

Enabling SNGs to contribute substantively to climate change action requires processes and skills in combining a national top-down perspective with a bottom-up component. National plans need to be disaggregated to show where they land over the national space, to allow for SNG efforts that can complement these. National plans ideally show where national resources are applied and how these plans dovetail with local plans, without being unduly directive or usurping SNG functions.

Both vertical and horizontal coordination is required, at all levels of government. Vertical integration refers to the alignment and coordination of climate policies, plans, and implementation across different levels of government, leveraging the potential of each respective level through collective efforts and promoting top-down and bottom-up information exchange. Vertical integration is facilitated by a well-chosen assignment of roles/functions related to climate change between levels of government. It entails building linkages between national and subnational adaptation planning, implementation, and monitoring and evaluation. While most times vertical integration is structured from the top-down, there can be instances of it being bottom-up, where actions and innovations at the local level inform policies and influence national plans that incorporate upscaling of successful local actions.

Horizontal integration entails coordination and cooperation across ministries and sectoral departments/units (of national and SNG levels) and can include non-state actors such as citizens' groups, private sector entities, and non-profits. Horizontal integration entails cooperation across units of an SNG and relevant interest groups to enable scale and encompass the benefits and costs of managing the ecosystem. Effectiveness in horizontal coordination across sectors at the subnational level enables the implementation of adaptation actions that are embedded in the development plans of the SNG. It is important then to ensure that, if there is a separate planning exercise for climate change action, the resulting plans are harmonized with the overall planning and budgeting process. This is where SNG planning for climate change often fails. As a recent report noted about the Viet Nam experience, "Climate change is currently poorly integrated into development plans, instead people tend to expect brand new projects with funding purely for climate change" (Strauch, Robiou du Pont, and Balanowski 2018). This view of climate change action tends to isolate projects, missing the opportunity to shape the bulk of development spending to contribute to lowering emissions and to add resilience against climate change risk.

The effectiveness of vertical and horizontal coordination contributes to the overall efficacy of multilevel governance. The effectiveness, as mentioned above, stems in part from the institutional arrangements of decentralized governance. The legal framework should allow SNGs to cooperate freely with other SNGs and development actors. Vertical linkages need to be in place for supervision but also support. The right to establish various forms of cooperation (vertical and horizontal, such as development forums and joint ventures) needs to be embedded in the organic/foundational law of SNGs. Some countries fail to provide for these possibilities and then try to add new institutions to advance climate change action. This may be workable, and needed, but can also add a burden to low-capacity SNGs that could be avoided by making the original institutional arrangements sufficiently robust and flexible to accommodate climate change action.

Some countries seek to give room for action to SNGs by adopting a functional assignment architecture that is replete with concurrent functions (where multiple levels can take on the same functions). Perhaps this is done with the hope that the combined efforts of several levels of government will add up to a significant and positive discharge of the function. But this approach to sharing functions bears a heavy cost of communication between all levels to check on which level should move forward or has moved forward, and how to assess the collective progress made against national objectives (DeLOG 2014).

The preparation of revised NDCs and of NAPs by national governments can serve as an opportunity to integrate the priorities of SNGs and their citizens, enabling ownership of the implementation process, horizontal and vertical linkage building, deliberations on reform pathways, collective priority setting, and collaborative resource mobilization. Conversely, draft or final SNG plans relevant to climate change action should find their way to the national level, to influence subsequent planning at this level, and to receive constructive guidance from a national perspective. The formulation of plans and commitments serves to include sectors and levels of government in comprehensive consultations not just for target setting but also to review subnational capacities, identify policy gaps, assess the efficacy of institutional arrangements, and consultatively identify institutional reforms that will allow for greater coherence and alignment in adaptation actions across sectors and scales of government.

Coherence in the planning and implementation of climate change action is also needed, both horizontally and vertically. This is not a straightforward procedure, as it requires communication and coordination at various stages in medium-term and annual planning processes and sharing information on implementation progress. Forums for reviewing draft plans and proposals are required, with appropriate degrees of involvement of stakeholders, but these need to be timely and not overly burdensome on participants. A national framework to guide regional/local planning on climate change is essential, and this must balance the need for guidance with the respect for regional/local autonomy that is built into the SNG legal framework. Box 6 presents the case of Nepal's Local Adaptation Plans for Action (LAPAs). Making draft and final versions of plans widely available to SNGs and citizens can help all assess whether there are consistencies and synergies across levels of government.

Post implementation, in the monitoring and evaluation phase, vertical coordination will enable capturing results and allow for feedback from the national to the subnational level and vice versa to be integrated into the next cycle of planning and implementation (Dazé, Price-Kelly, and Rass 2016). In the case of Nepal's LAPA initiative, the feedback pointed to the need for a national policy to act as an umbrella for LAPAs, and to integrate LAPAs in a tighter way into the intergovernmental framework that was evolving as Nepal shifted to a federal structure. The success noted thus far in LAPA implementation tends to owe to projects funded by various bilateral and multilateral funds. This remained the case even against the background of Nepal's 2009 Climate Change Policy, which mandated that 80% of all climate adaptation finance be utilized at the local level (Practical Action 2024). The success of LAPAs then rides on the ability of the government to realize the fiscal decentralization objectives embedded in its shift to a federal structure that was meant to empower SNGs in terms of mandates and resources.

Box 6: Integrating Local Adaptation Plans of Action in Nepal

As one of its responses to its vulnerabilities to climate change, in 2011 Nepal created a national framework to guide the preparation of Local Adaptation Plans of Action (LAPAs) with the objectives of (i) implementing adaptation actions, and (ii) assimilating climate change into local development planning and implementation. The framework guided the incorporation of climate change action in sectoral and comprehensive development plans. LAPAs are prepared by village development committees and municipalities—the lowest administrative units in Nepal, operating beneath the district level. The framework was designed as a participatory process that involved local communities analyzing vulnerability to climate change and prioritizing adaptation actions for their locality. These local plans were then integrated into development plans at district and national levels through an iterative process. The seven steps in LAPA were climate change sensitization, climate vulnerability and adaptation assessment, prioritization of adaptation options, LAPA formulation, integration into planning processes, implementation, and progress assessment.

The LAPA process has been unique in piloting and demonstrating a bottom-up, inclusive, community-driven approach that is integrated upward into the National Adaptation Plan of Action. As of 2016, 93 LAPAs for village development committees and 7 LAPAs for municipalities were prepared and implemented in 14 of the most climate-vulnerable districts. This has provided lessons relevant to countries seeking to institutionalize an upward flow in climate change action planning.

- Local adaptation actions are very limited in their ambitions. They aid in piloting bottom-up approaches, building capacities, and generating awareness but cannot be expected to address larger climate-related challenges. Implementation also needs to enable community and frontline functionaries to distinguish adaptation investments from mainstream development activity.
- The focus on vertical integration must be complemented by robust horizontal integration mechanisms to enable scale and allow leveraging strengths and opportunities across diverse stakeholders.
- While the absence of scientific knowledge at such scales can be an issue, efforts need to be made to gather and build a repository of indigenous knowledge on materials, construction methods, sowing patters, raw materials, climate indicators, etc.
- Assessing the effectiveness of implemented adaptation in improving local resilience requires significant technical support and handholding of local communities.
- Local government's ability to work with local multistakeholder institutional mechanisms requires agreements across line ministries to modify task descriptions, institutionalize new collaborative mechanisms at the local level, rework reporting arrangements, and incentivize horizontal collaboration across sectors as well as non-state actors.

With the rewriting of the Constitution and the shift to a federal state, the LAPA approach has been revised to match the federal governance architecture, and the revised framework focuses on integrating LAPA into municipalities' planning and budgeting processes.

Sources: Government of Nepal. 2011. National Framework on Local Adaptation Plans for Action; Global Water Partnership. 2017. *Nepal's Approach to Climate Change Adaptation with Local Adaptation Plans for Action (LAPAs): A Water Resource Perspective*; R. Ghimire and N. Chhetri. 2022. Challenges and Prospects of Local Adaptation Plans of Action (LAPA) Initiative in Nepal as Everyday Adaptation. *Ecology and Society*. 27 (4).

2. Institutional Arrangements That Aid Horizontal Alignment

It is often the case that national governments demand that SNGs take up new themes that correspond to emerging national interests or commitments made in the context of global forums. To name a few themes, SNGs have been asked to weave into their policies and plans the themes of poverty alleviation, reducing stunting in children, reducing vulnerability to natural hazards, managing their impact, and responding to the coronavirus disease pandemic. This horizontal integration of new themes into the regular policy/planning streams of SNGs is not easy to bring about, and time is always an issue. Addressing climate change at SNG level is no different in this regard. Integrating it effectively requires SNGs to (i) mandate a coordinating institution with sufficient authority and autonomy, (ii) set up adaptation units in departments of vulnerable sectors, and (iii) set up an interdepartmental task force to facilitate exchange and collaborative working. While such institutional arrangements are common, issues emerge when they are project-specific and are discontinued at the end of project life. This can happen when external funders impose dedicated project structures rather than working with and enhancing existing structures. It requires investments to be made to institutionalize and make sustainable successful working protocols (Clar and Steurer 2019). The case from a state in India in Box 7 presents an understanding of the contribution that horizontal integration across agencies in the livestock sector could make in strengthening climate resilience for livestock-rearing communities.

The institutional changes shown in the case of Madhya Pradesh are significant and may not be feasible or relevant for many state and rural SNGs. However, for larger rural SNGs and for regional SNG such changes could be within reach, or capacity could be developed to bring about such institutional transformations that are sustainable (and not project-driven or required simply to meet donor/financier requirements). Naturally, before this degree of institutional modification, it is advisable to undertake a comprehensive institutional analysis to understand the scope of changes needed to improve vertical and horizontal coordination across sectors in matters related to climate change.

3. Institutional Arrangements That Aid Vertical Alignment

Vertical alignment that is consistent with SNG autonomy is challenging to construct. Top-down instructions are ruled out in this case, and it is therefore important to find platforms and incentives that will induce communication, negotiation, coordination, and collaboration. One of the ways to do this is through formal platforms of inclusiveness, such as cross-government and multistakeholder platforms to discuss development issues. These have been constructed in several countries to push toward achievement of the SDGs.

Another institutional approach to solving the coordination problem is through the "dual function" design of the regional executive, as found in several countries, like Indonesia and Pakistan. The SNG head (of the executive) wears two hats: the (usually elected) executive head of the SNG and representative of the national government. The executive leader (e.g., governor), when acting as a representative of the national/central government, can in principle be the focal point for harmonizing policies and adapting national programs to the needs of the regions. In Indonesia, this role has not been fully fleshed out until recently, and is still short on how it is put into practice organizationally (e.g., how autonomous regional units fit into the picture), but in terms of regulations the governors

Box 7: Improving Climate Resilience in the Animal Husbandry Sector in Madhya Pradesh Through Strengthened Horizontal Coordination Across Agencies

India is a federal country, hence key sectors related to climate change are primarily state subjects. States have prepared their State Action Plans for Climate Change (SAPCCs) since 2009, to be funded from their sector budgets. Madhya Pradesh, a state in central India, set up the State Knowledge Management Centre on Climate Change (SKMCCC) to prepare the SAPCC, consisting of sector working groups to undertake vulnerability assessments. Members were provided with training, tools, and linkages to experts. After the formulation of the SAPCC in 2013, SKMCCC supported sector departments in mainstreaming adaptation in existing initiatives and in suggesting new programs.

Observing a decline in milk yield, the Department of Animal Husbandry researched the causes as part of the vulnerability assessments required for preparing the SAPCC. The decline was attributed to increasing temperatures that were affecting the exotic and cross-breed cows. Rising temperatures affected food availability, quality, and body temperatures of the high-yielding cows, resulting in declining milk yields. Consequently, the department has initiated efforts to incentivize indigenous breeds of capital, investing in climate-resilient breeding programs, capacity building of vets and para-vets, stepping up monitoring efforts to track the progress of the shift to indigenous breed, improving insurance coverage, and investing in improving fodder yields.

Success in integrating adaptation in the regular programming of the department was enabled by (i) the entry point provided by the SAPCC preparation—along with background information—for the department to further assess vulnerabilities; (ii) political support, which has also enabled finance availability; (iii) horizontal coordination with the livestock and poultry development corporation and the state dairy federation to validate findings, consult on policy improvements, and enable outreach; (iv) the capacity development investments made by SKMCCC through knowledge provisioning and linking with experts far beyond the reach of the department, (v) collaborations with State Disaster Management Authority and Agriculture Training Institute that the department forged to roll out a training and outreach program; and (vi) repurposing of departmental funds, which received approvals owing to political support and the systematic evidence put forth in support of the proposal.

Sources: A. Dinshaw et al. 2018. Mainstreaming Adaptation in Action: Case Studies from Two States in India. *Working Paper*. World Resources Institute; S. Bhatt et al. 2019. India: NAPCC Process Country Case Study. GIZ.

have been strengthened in their supervisory and support roles toward districts and cities. For instance, the governor is to lead the province and district/cities in the preparation of the Action Plan on the SDGs (Ferrazzi 2023). A similar approach could also work to link national and regional/local climate change action planning where this dual function design is found in the state architecture.

The need to meet global commitments within stipulated time frames can lead national governments to compromise on the consultative processes that enable the inclusion of SNG priorities, concerns, and contributions. In many NDCs around the world, there is no explicit mention of the role SNGs play in achieving national climate goals (ICLEI 2018). This is beginning to change, and the pace of subnational involvement in NDC preparation may gain momentum (NDC 3.0 Navigator 2024). The institutionalized inclusion and engagement of SNGs in the formative stages of policy development, plan preparation, and target setting allows for more realistic policy framing, target setting, and assessment of resource needs and challenges. Along with promoting ownership and commitment of the lower levels of government, it also improves preparedness for implementation. Alongside, it allows for local constraints and challenges to be factored into more realistic goal setting by SNGs, sets the basis for a better coordinated effort, and spells a better chance at coherence in implementation efforts (Christoplos et al. 2016).

4. Clarifying and Tracking Climate Change Action Expenditures

To translate national policies into concrete action on climate change, it is important to have a way of discerning expenditures supportive of this aim. Toward this end, some countries in the Asia and the Pacific are investing in budget tagging,[16] recognizing that this tool may help SNGs monitor climate-related financial flows, facilitate assessment of the adequacy and appropriateness of climate funding, and improve transparency and accountability. In Asia and the Pacific, five out of the eight countries (Table 3) that have introduced climate-based tagging have included SNGs in their coverage. Box 8 discusses how the effort is unfolding in the Philippines; progress is being made but challenges persist.

Table 3: Overview of Progress in Climate Budget Tagging in Asia and the Pacific

Country	Subnational Transfers/Budgets	Coverage	Budget Type	Tagging
Bangladesh	Yes	SS	I & R	C
Cambodia (limited to aid database)		SS	I & R	C
India (pilot)		SS	I	C
Indonesia		SS	I & R	LA
Nepal	Yes	AS	I	LA
Pakistan	Yes	SS	I & R	C
Philippines	Yes	AS	I & R	LA
Thailand			I & R	LA
Viet Nam	Yes	SS	I & R	

AS = all sectors, C = centralized, I = investment, LA = line agency, R = recurrent, SS = selected sectors.

Source: L. Baumgartner, R. Carman, and Y. Liu. 2022. *The State of Climate Ambition, Regional Snapshot Asia and the Pacific*. UNDP.

16 Climate budget tagging is defined as a tool for identifying, classifying, weighting, and marking climate-relevant expenditures in a government's budget system, enabling the estimation, monitoring, and tracking of those expenditures; see UNDP (2019a).

Box 8: Budget Tracking Through Tagging in the Philippines

The Philippines reports quantitative metrics for adaptation at the local level and tracks both total amount and percentage of finance for adaptation at the national and municipal levels. The Department of Budget Management is responsible for budget tagging at the national level, while local government units (LGUs) are responsible for budget tagging at the local level, and the national Climate Change Commission assesses and ensures the quality of the climate tagging. There is a six-digit typology code that includes an adaptation or mitigation marker (A or M); three digits for the strategic priority, sub-priority, and instrument; and a two-digit activity code. Adaptation codes include space to denote which of four instruments is being funded through the local budget: (i) policy development and governance; (ii) research, development, and extension; (iii) knowledge sharing and capacity building; and (iv) service delivery.

LGUs are also responsible for planning and implementing climate actions in their communities; Local Climate Change Action Plans are integrated with Local Development Plans, the National Framework Strategy on Climate Change, and the National Climate Change Action Plan. Each municipality publishes an annual investment program brief that includes the total number and funding amount of climate change adaptation and climate change mitigation investments, funding source, and alignment of these investments with the National Climate Change Action Plan. The Department of the Interior and Local Government is meant to provide continuous capacity-building programs for LGUs to institutionalize and sustain climate change expenditure tracking in LGU annual investment programming and budget planning processes.

Despite consistent efforts, there are areas for further improvement. Budget tagging is based on a list of pro-climate expenditures (mainly adaptation) but is yet to include the negative impact of expenditures on climate change (e.g., fuel subsidies). It also needs to consider the tax incentives and assess their impact on the climate transition. Compliance with budget tagging is still low.

Sources: T. Coger et al. 2021. Tracking and Reporting Finance for Locally Led Adaptation to Climate Change. Working Paper. World Resources Institute; World Bank. 2022b. *Philippines Country Climate and Development Report*.

Having expenditure data can help track the consistency of implementation with policies. In OECD countries, it is known that SNGs are responsible for 63% of climate-significant public expenditure and 69% of climate-significant public investment. Yet, even in this region, researchers admit that "only limited evidence exists to establish how much SNGs spend and invest on climate change, and if their sources of revenue can fund the needs of the green transition" (OECD 2022a). Budget tagging can support broader expenditure analysis that underpins broad greening strategies. For instance, Climate Policy Expenditure and Institutional Reviews (UNDP 2019b) have been attempted in several countries in Asia and the Pacific.[17] In some countries in this region, they have been undertaken at the subnational level, such as in India (in the states of Bihar, Chhattisgarh, and Kerala), Indonesia, and Nepal (Martinez-Vasquez 2021). These exercises have enabled the tracking of climate spending at the subnational level, strengthened climate finance management capacities, and aided subnational entities to advocate for sector-specific adaptation resources (UNDP 2022).

[17] Countries in Asia and the Pacific using this tool include Bangladesh, Cambodia, Indonesia, Nepal, the Philippines, Samoa, Thailand, and Viet Nam.

Achieving the commitments made in the Paris Agreement and other green objectives would require greater understanding of the financial roles and authorities of SNGs so that their expenditures, investments, and revenues can be aligned with their climate goals. Acknowledging this, OECD launched the Subnational Government Climate Finance Hub ("the Hub") in 2022 (Box 9). Unfortunately, even the scarce OECD data would be a high bar for SNGs in Asia and the Pacific. Most countries in this region have yet to classify their climate change expenditures at SNG level, and region-wide collaboration on this effort has yet to get off the ground. This lag in data will impede the green budget approach that is emerging, under this label or other associated practices including carbon budgets, ecoBudgets, climate budgets, and environmental and climate impact analyses (OECD 2022b).

Box 9: The Organisation for Economic Co-operation and Development Subnational Government Climate Finance Hub

The Organisation for Economic Co-operation and Development (OECD) Hub or "the Hub" was launched in 2022, in the framework of a joint project between the OECD and the European Commission Directorate-General for Regional and Urban Policy on "Measuring and Enhancing Subnational Government Finance for Environment and Climate Action in OECD and EU Countries."

The Hub seeks to compile outputs from the OECD/European Commission data gathering on the topic of subnational climate finance, structuring them around three main pillars: at the macro level, it covers subnational climate expenditure tracking and subnational climate revenue tracking; at the micro level, it dives more granularly into the topic of subnational green budgeting.

Source: www.oecd.org/en/about/programmes/subnational-government-climate-finance-hub.html.

C. Autonomy in Revenue Raising and Borrowing for Climate Change Action

Investing in climate-resilient infrastructure and the diverse range of other actions requires significant additional financing. The International Monetary Fund estimates that investments needed for climate-proofing infrastructure average 3.3% of gross domestic product per annum for Asia and the Pacific (Fouad et al. 2020). As this report explains, most of these investments fall, or could fall, under the jurisdiction of SNGs. Unfortunately, estimated adaptation cost/needs alone are currently between 5 and 10 times higher than international adaptation finance flows, widening the adaptation finance gap (UNEP 2022). Most countries of the region must rely on substantial foreign sources of finance even to keep investment at current levels. In East Asia and the Pacific, in the past decade, 93% has been raised domestically while 7% has been from international sources. By comparison, South Asia raised 43% domestically while 57% was raised internationally (Naran et al. 2022). Own revenues of SNGs in Asia and the Pacific are thus constrained by the overall government domestic revenues.

Financial data specific to subnational revenues is not always available or reliable. The OECD and ADB (2023) estimate that SNGs in Asia and the Pacific collect about 35% of total government revenues, and that SNGs account for 7.4% of total public debt, but there is much variation across countries. The share of SNG revenue in total public revenue is highest in countries in South and Southeast Asia. It is lower in countries in Central and West Asia, on average. This OECD/ADB review of a 26-country sample also noted that 4 countries banned SNGs from borrowing and 7 countries limited SNGs to borrowing from public financial institutions.

SNG borrowing in the form of bonds is in early stages of development in Asia and the Pacific. In 14 out of 26 countries covered in the OECD/ADB study, regulations were permissive, yet SNGs rarely issued bonds. Subnational bond markets are not well developed and SNGs may not be deemed sufficiently creditworthy (OECD and ADB 2023). Here, the low level of SNG own revenue mobilization encourages the view in the market that SNGs are not financially solid enough to issue bonds.

Domestically, in most countries the primary ways to raise revenue for SNGs are (i) locally levied charges, which usually consist of property tax and land development tax, at a rate fixed by the central government, and user fees for specifically assigned services (often referred to as own-source revenue); (ii) shared taxes (such as goods and services tax), which are collected nationally and shared between the local and the central government; and (iii) grants received from the central government. Intergovernmental fiscal transfers from national governments (items ii and iii) constitute the largest ratio of receipts in the subnational and local government budget.

The high dependence of SNGs on transfers reflects the lack of revenue assignments to SNGs, the freedom of SNGs to set their own rates, and low enforcement capacities. The dominance of transfers also means that SNGs are tied to conditions as to what they can spend; these conditional grants are usually larger than unconditional grants. The conditionalities can restrict the fiscal autonomy of SNGs and keep them from prioritizing mitigation or adaptation spending in line with local needs. They also imply limited autonomy and flexibility to tailor solutions to local climate impacts and leave little possibility to channel resources during a crisis (Yap, Cociña, and Levy 2021).

SNG action on climate change is not always dependent on rich coffers. SNGs can choose to regulate the public and private sectors, thus influencing behavior. Moreover, even small local charges can have a nudge effect. For instance, parking charges can encourage the use of public transport. They can also influence behavior via fairly modest expenditures on awareness-raising campaigns. SNGs can also mobilize community efforts to accomplish some climate change action. Nonetheless, the reality is that the low levels of own-source revenue of SNGs severely limit ambitious and locally owned climate change initiatives.

While the generally low level of local revenues raised by SNGs in countries in Asia and the Pacific is holding back efforts in climate change action, the flipside of this argument is that there is much scope for raising local funds if more effort is made. To begin with, it is worth noting that citizens are often paying for climate change actions themselves, meaning that they recognize the value of these actions and leave open the possibility of a more efficient collective response—one that shares the burden more equitably among citizens. The case of Bangladesh in disaster preparedness and response shows how significant that can be (Box 10).

Box 10: Rural Household Spending on Disaster Preparedness in Bangladesh

A study by the International Institute for Environment and Development in Bangladesh published in 2019 concluded that rural households in Bangladesh spent almost $2 billion on disaster preparedness and response (e.g., repairs and saving for emergency needs), which was more than double the national government's climate and disaster spending.

The research also revealed that households headed by women spent three times more than those headed by men on climate and disaster preparedness. The study undertaken again after 2 years using primary data once more revealed that not only were poor rural households most affected by climate-related risks but also they spent as much as 15% of their total household expenditure on risk reduction. This is even higher for households headed by women, which are spending as much as 30% of their household expenditure, double that of households headed by men. The 2021 study found similar figures, with the estimates hovering at about $1.7 billion per year.

Sources: S. Eskander and S. Steele. 2019. Bearing the Climate Burden: How Households in Bangladesh Are Spending Too Much. Issue Paper. IIED; S. Eskander et al. 2022. Still Bearing the Burden: How Poor Rural Women in Bangladesh Are Paying Most for Climate Risks. Working Paper. IIED.

SNGs can tap into this evident willingness to address climate change risk. It may also be possible for SNGs to tap into the high individual/family giving that characterizes communal solidarity in some countries of Asia and the Pacific. For instance, Indonesia has placed as the most generous country in the world for the fifth year in a row (to 2022). During 2021, more than 8 in 10 people donated money and more than 6 in 10 (63%) volunteered time (CAF 2022). SNGs may need to find ways to convince citizens that climate change action is consistent with their faith and personal preferences, resulting in more SNG–civil society partnerships and greater willingness to pay taxes for SNG-managed expenditures and projects.

D. Intergovernmental Transfers to Enhance the Fiscal Capacity of Subnational Governments

As in many countries around the world, in many countries of Asia and the Pacific the national government collects more revenue than it spends and must devise a set of intergovernmental fiscal transfer mechanisms to channel funds to SNGs to carry out their assigned functions, particularly if these functions are labeled as obligatory/mandated functions. In this region, grants are the primary source of SNG revenue (48%), slightly below the global and OECD averages of 52% and 53%, respectively (OECD and ADB 2023).

The use of intergovernmental grants reflects alignment in its most basic sense: funding is provided to SNGs (from national revenues or shared revenues) to avoid that all too pervasive pitfall of decentralization—unfunded mandates. Unfunded mandates can lead to inaction or inadequate responses to local challenges, as seen recently in the coronavirus response, where it is suggested that unfunded mandates of SNGs led to higher mortality rates (Andrés Rodríguez-Pose and Vidal-Bover 2023).

Addressing vertical fiscal imbalances can lead to reliance on transfers and hence spending that is constrained by national government-imposed conditionalities. In South Asian countries such as Bangladesh, India, and Nepal, transfer systems have become more complex, with conditional transfers made through centrally formulated programs. Programs have their own procedures and conditions on planning, spending, and reporting, and provide little discretion on spending by the local governments. In contrast, in countries of Southeast Asia such as Indonesia and the Philippines, the conditional transfers to SNGs are more stable, predictable, and transparent, creating better conditions for SNGs to plan their climate-proofing investments even when conditionalities constrain them. However, where SNG proposals are required to access these grants, sometimes with requirements to be matched by local funds, then even in these countries, cities and larger rural SNGs (e.g., districts in Indonesia and municipalities in the Philippines) tend to win out as a result of their greater capacities to pull together convincing proposals, or their tighter bonds with higher-level decision makers.

Whereas intergovernmental transfers are a common feature of SNGs in Asia and the Pacific, climate change action-specific transfers are not yet common and do not yet represent a significant proportion of the transfers. Some countries are beginning to explore the concept of, or have moved forward with, the greening of intergovernmental grants (Table 4). Some of these grants are for a variety of environmental activities, but most do directly or indirectly support climate change mitigation and adaptation.

The creation of ecological fiscal transfers/climate change action transfers holds some promise (Loft, Gebara, and Wong 2016). These transfers are meant to compensate SNGs for the costs of conserving ecosystems and the opportunity costs foregone from pursuing alternative revenue-generating activities. While they are conditional grants—which reduces SNG discretion—they can help align SNG efforts with national policies and targets on climate change action. Although some of these transfers (e.g., for Indonesia and the Republic of Korea) are not exclusively focused on climate change, the transfers can be used for projects that have climate-related benefits. As noted in the discussion earlier on budget tracking, one could probe other sector/thematic transfers (e.g., health, environment) to find components that are also supportive of climate change action, leading to the conundrum of how to classify SNG expenditures on climate change action.

Where climate change action-related transfers are built into shared revenue mechanisms, or are placed alongside these, they may serve to offset the negative incentives arising from resource extraction shared revenues, which tend to encourage the expansion of extraction activities. In practice, it is hard to tell the net effect of extraction versus climate change measures. More broadly, there is still little evidence to show that these climate change-related transfers have a significant impact on meeting national/SNG carbon emission targets or other indicators (e.g., forest cover). More research will be needed to determine whether SNGs spend more on climate change action as a result of receiving these grants and whether their actions yield results.

Table 4: Climate Change-Oriented Intergovernmental Transfers in Asia and the Pacific

Country	Intergovernmental Transfer Description	Development/Status	Scale of Funds
People's Republic of China	A performance-based program for local nature conservation and abatement of local environmental pollution to motivate local authorities to improve eco-environmental quality	Initiated in 2008, primarily used to lower pollution but also to improve environmental quality. The transfer used is the main transfer to SNGs, with ecological indicators. There are central-to-provincial and provincial-to-county mechanisms.	CNY79.45 billion in 2020 for national to provincial (about $11 billion): 1.14% of all transfers
India	Intergovernmental fiscal transfers to the state level focused on conservation, protection, and restoration of water bodies and forests	Development began with 14th Finance Commission (2013), which integrated climate change as one of the criteria to determine the intergovernmental fiscal transfers to the states.	10% of the tax share of the divisible pool of taxes to SNGs
Indonesia	Fiscal transfer mechanism called "ecological fiscal transfers," which includes elements related to climate change mitigation, particularly forest conservation	Built into existing transfers; "incentive transfer" for waste management and "special transfer" for the environment and forestry. Piloting underway for transfers from province to districts/cities and from districts to villages.	Small; less than 5% of transfers (from national level)
Philippines	People's Survival Fund provides finance for adaptation projects of local government and local/community organizations aimed at increasing the resilience of communities and ecosystems to climate change	Established in 2012 through a separate Act. It is managed by a separate Board led by the Department of Finance.	Annually at least ₱1 billion (very small compared with ₱871 billion received by local government unit)
Viet Nam	Working on integrating climate change considerations into its intergovernmental fiscal transfer system	The country has been developing a framework for climate change-related transfers to support local-level climate action, particularly for adaptation projects in vulnerable regions.	Not yet implemented

SNG = subnational government.

Sources: Author's review of country mechanisms and estimates and Strauch, Robiou du Pont, and Balanowski (2018), Rahman (2019), Chakraborty (2021), Climate Change Commission (2024), and Liu, Xiong, and Zhang (2024).

IV. Accessing Global Resources to Support Climate Change Action by Subnational Governments

A. Accessing Climate Financing for Subnational Government Climate Change Action

In 2017, ADB estimated that infrastructure needs in developing Asia and the Pacific would rise to over $26 trillion, or $1.7 trillion per year when climate change mitigation and adaptation costs are incorporated. While government hopes for a growing private sector and civil society contribution, for the medium term the burden of this investment and related climate change action expenditures will need to come from the public sector. Worldwide public sector financing of climate change action grew by nearly 10% annually over the decade 2011–2020 (Figure 2). Climate financing is fragmented, with national funds and multiple multilateral and bilateral institutions lending/granting making significant contributions. Global funds are highly visible in the public discourse but contribute a rather modest amount compared with national and multilateral and bilateral institutions. The various institutions involved bring to their work varying standards and practices (Weikmans and Timmons Roberts 2019). It is therefore difficult to be definitive about the magnitude and nature of these flows.

One estimate suggests that about a quarter of total climate finance in the period from 2016 to 2020 was adaptation finance (OECD 2022c). Climate finance has tended to flow to a few regions of the world. For instance, East Asia (especially the PRC) has shown large investments in key sectors such as electric vehicles and solar energy. Regions where the majority of low- and middle-income countries are located received less than 25% of climate finance flows. The breakdown of financing by national and subnational level has not been systematically tracked beyond OECD countries.

Despite increasing recognition of the importance of subnational actors in climate governance, the actual allocation of financial resources derived from global (transnational) funds remains skewed toward national governments. The extent of this skew is hard to determine. The Local Governments and Municipal Authorities (LGMA)[18] Constituency of the UNFCCC has advocated for multilevel climate change action but its success in highlighting cases of city/region efforts has yet to lead to a system of data collection that would shine light on how much climate financing they are receiving. It is clear that adaptation measures are largely locally financed. Global climate change funds are highly visible, but they still constitute only a minor share—roughly 9%—of total public adaptation finance (Canales and Savvidou 2023). The vast majority is spent by national and subnational governments,

---

18 The LGMA Constituency represents networks of local and regional governments under the UNFCCC.

Figure 2: Climate Finance from Different Sources Within the Public Sector
($ billion)

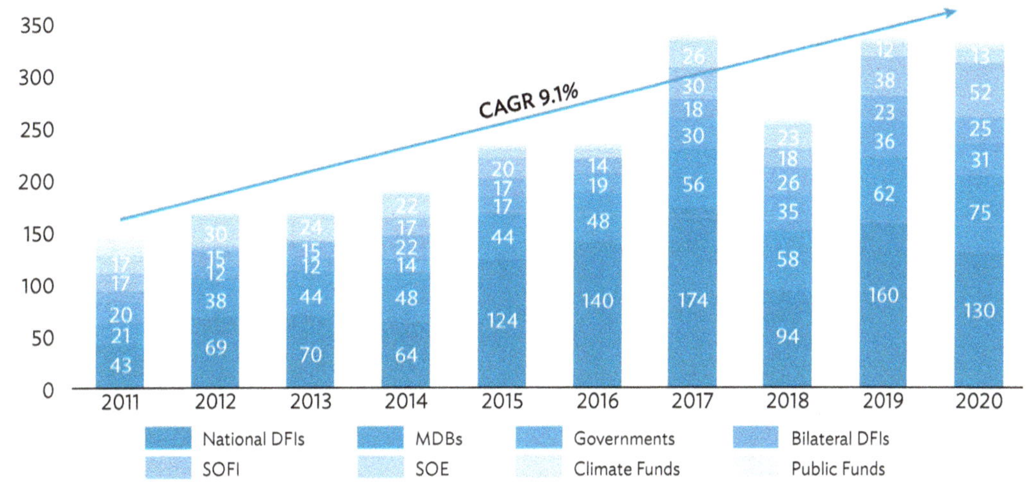

CAGR = compound annual growth rate, DFI = development finance institution, MDB = multilateral development bank, SOE = state-owned enterprise, SOFI = smart organic food initiative.

Source: B. Naran et al. (2022). *Global Landscape of Climate Finance: A Decade of Data 2011-2020.* Climate Policy Initiative.

with the latter depending for its funding largely on intergovernmental transfers (Mitroliou 2018). As already indicated in the discussion on intergovernmental transfers, the emergence of climate change action components in these granting systems is still in the nascent stage.

One of the developments in climate finance in recent years has been the establishment of national funds that are funded by the national government but often include a contribution from donors or international finance institutions. These can have various governance structures, but they are generally sitting outside of the intergovernmental transfer systems. For example, the Indonesia Climate Change Trust Fund (ICCTF) is governed by a board of trustees chaired by Bappenas (the Ministry of National Development Planning) and has the Bank Mandiri as the trustee (Bhandary 2024). One of the goals of the ICCTF is to integrate climate change issues into national, provincial, and district development plans. The ICCTF channels funds from the World Bank to its activities, combining these with national funds. Over the period 2010–2022, it funded 115 projects, with 13 others ongoing as of 2022 (ICCTF 2024). While these projects (e.g., in marine conservation) are dispersed throughout Indonesia's provinces, and provincial staff take part in some activities, it is not clear what the level of ownership of the participating SNG is in these projects, and whether they lead to better plans and investments at SNG level. There is inertia in national governments and external funders in moving away from centralized approaches, even when the functions and interests of SNGs are at stake.

National climate funds can help fill capacity gaps (a task not suited to most intergovernmental transfers) and enable countries to eventually formulate specialized policy instruments. They can also positively impact distributional aspects of addressing climate change if the fund includes this as one of its objectives (Bhandary 2024). Examples of these include the Bangladesh Climate Change Trust

Fund, the Bangladesh Local Disaster Risk Reduction Fund, the Bangladesh Climate Change Resilience Fund, and the Cambodia Climate Change Alliance, which provides pools of resources for the mainstreaming of climate change into national and subnational programs. In Asia and the Pacific, there are as many as 24 national climate funds set up. Bangladesh, India, and Indonesia have more than one such fund. National climate funds can potentially channel international climate finance to SNGs that are unable to directly access global finance.

Global funds are smaller than national funds but have shown moderate growth over the past decade. The four largest multilateral climate funds are the Adaptation Fund (AF), the Climate Investment Funds (CIF), the Global Environment Facility (GEF), and the Green Climate Fund (GCF). Table 5 shows their accessibility for SNGs.

Table 5: Access to Multilateral Climate Funds for Subnational Governments

Global Fund	Size	How the Fund Works	SNG Access
AF	2010–2023: $323 million for 54 projects in 31 countries in Asia and the Pacific (31% of the Fund)	Proposals are made directly through accredited national, regional, or multilateral implementing entities.	It is in principle possible for SNGs to become accredited national implementing agencies, but not clear if it is done. The current list does not show any SNGs.
CIF	In Asia, 106 projects for $2.4 billion, attracting $21 billion in cofinancing	Channels concessional finance through MDBs for advisory and investment activities, based on country/MDB expression of interest and investment plan	Access of SNGs depends on MDB's ability and willingness to make SNGs executing or implementing agencies for their financed projects. CIF has an Indigenous Peoples and local community window but this is not necessarily linked to SNGs.
GEF Trust Funds	Programmed $495.6 million (about $65 million being climate change) in 2024, plus $5.84 billion in cofinancing. Breakdown for Asia and the Pacific not provided.	18 GEF agencies execute the program (e.g., UNDP, UNEP, UNIDO, World Bank, FAO). Partnerships with WRI, C40 Cities, and ICLEI – Local Governments for Sustainability are used to approach cities.	Sustainable Cities Integrated Program has involved Malaysia, the Philippines, and Sri Lanka in integrating urban planning, implementing policies, and investing in nature-positive, climate-resilient, and carbon-neutral urban development. SNGs' role in relation to GEF executing agencies is not clear.
GCF	$14.9 billion for 269 projects across 129 countries	Proposal-based, arising from national designated authority or focal point	It is in principle possible for SNGs to become accredited national implementing agencies, but not clear if it is done. Current list does not show any SNGs.

AF = Adaptation Fund, CIF = Climate Investment Funds, FAO = Food and Agriculture Organization of the United Nations, GCF = Green Climate Fund, GEF = Global Environment Facility, MDB = multilateral development bank, SNG = subnational government, UNDP = United Nations Development Programme, UNEP = United Nations Environment Programme, UNIDO = United Nations Industrial Development Organization, WRI = World Resources Institute.

Source: Author's analysis of web-based information provided by global funds (AF 2023, CIF 2024, GEF 2024).

Given that the channeling of MDB, national, and global funds is not generally through SNGs, the funds that are directed from these sources to SNGs—and managed by SNGs—remain small compared with intergovernmental grants or SNGs' own-source revenue. Moreover, national, global, and MDB funding is allocated based on criteria that do not include equalizing SNG resources horizontally. While the needs will vary across SNGs, most SNGs face climate change impacts and aspire to address these. There also appears to be inequity across regions in the allocation of global funds, with the share going to Asia and the Pacific falling short of the population represented by the region. In this respect, climate change funding may be following the broader pattern of official development assistance, which is driven by numerous factors. To be definitive on this point would require more disaggregated climate change funding data reporting by the global funds.

This assessment is tentative as the global funds do not make it easy in their presentations and documents to discern how much funding is directed to projects that are managed by SNGs themselves. Where explanation is given, it seems that MDBs or other international actors (e.g., GEF agencies) take the lead role, and merely involve SNGs. The ownership, control, and capacity generated in the SNG are thus difficult to assess. There is not a clear intent or set of modalities (e.g., a SNG window) in the global funds to balance national and SNG interventions in a way that might reflect the state's assignment of functions. As an example, in a recent GCF initiative in Malaysia, the focus of institutional strengthening in the preparation of the NAP is national government agencies; state governments are deemed indirect beneficiaries that could draw lessons from how the NAP is prepared and conducted for any eventual NAP they might undertake (GCF 2024a). This is a lost opportunity to give the states a more active role and make the eventual NAP more likely to see consistent implementation, as well as to form a more appropriate umbrella for any future state-level NAP.

The proposal-based approaches that dominate access paths to global fund resources work against SNGs in comparison with national governments and are inequitable across SNGs. Attaining accreditation to channel global fund resources may also be more difficult for SNGs—but it is not clear whether this has been tested. Projects from global funds find their way to the local level, but they may rest on community/Indigenous Peoples participation rather than SNG-led approaches or combined community–SNG approaches. It is not clear that SNGs' advantages in local knowledge and networks are utilized to optimize community engagement. For instance, SNG institutions may be important in land use planning/cadasters, which is a crucial element of community-level efforts to gain community involvement in conservation or social forestry. Involving the SNG is also usually the most sensible way of scaling up an approach. Insufficient engagement of SNGs in the small-scale and direct-to-community/Indigenous Peoples grants/support provided by international or national actors reduces the potential of subsequent scaling-up and institutionalization.

The channeling of funds through national designated authorities (NDAs) can be an efficient mechanism for global funds. However, this intermediary role of the NDA (e.g., played by the Ministry of Finance in Indonesia for the GCF) could result in an inequitable distribution of funds in the absence of objective criteria for decision-making that takes into account the severity of challenges faced by SNGs and their funding gaps. Also, there is a risk of conscious and unconscious bias in decision-making. The ensuing resource distribution could then hinder the ability of SNGs to implement climate actions that are responsive to local needs and vulnerabilities. Smaller, less networked, and poorly resourced SNGs are at a particular disadvantage, as their relationship with the NDAs is likely more tenuous than is the case for larger city/regional governments. Notwithstanding these potential pitfalls, national funds could serve to attract global funding and to distribute this equitably. The GCF has accredited the Cambodian National Committee for Subnational Democratic Development (NCDD) Secretariat to receive finance directly to engage SNGs in adaptation activities. The NCDD is concerned with the equitable development of all SNGs in Cambodia and is well placed to ensure funds fit with the assignment of functions—a decentralization exercise it has led over the past decade or more. It is still too early to assess the extent to which these facilities are successful in channeling resources to SNGs (Patel et al. 2020).

Where accreditation is open to nongovernment entities, it is possible to find nongovernment organizations that are capable and dedicated to their concerns, but again they may not be comfortable or interested in working closely with SNGs. The Partnership for Governance Reform in Indonesia is an accredited body in Indonesia for the GCF and has been approved for funding to prepare a project in flood resiliency in Central Java. The involvement of the province and districts/cities in the watershed of interest comes as consultation at the beginning and end of the project (GCF 2024b). This does not bode well for sustainability.

Direct access to global climate funds is largely ruled out by accreditation thresholds to gain access to global funds (that require substantial public financial management capacity) and national rules that centralize flows of external financing. Their uncertain fiscal management capabilities, low absorptive capacity, and weak horizontal linkages place these SNGs at a disadvantage in accessing global finances. In one analysis of climate change projects approved in 2003–2016, less than 10% of climate finance from global climate funds was dedicated to local actions. While there are as many as 99 climate funds listed in the database maintained by the Climate Fund Update, most of these are skewed toward supporting national efforts that promise scale in impact (Soanes et al. 2017).

From the perspective of global climate funds, entertaining proposals directly from local entities is onerous given (i) the high transaction costs of administering small projects, (ii) assessment metrics of global funds that are better suited to large mitigation projects that report on tons of carbon reduced, (iii) difficulty faced by SNGs in presenting relevant evidence to demonstrate management capabilities and fiscal discipline as climate funds usually look to support entities that have successful mobilized cofinance from one or more other sources, (iv) SNGs lacking horizontal linkages and ways to work at a larger scale, and (v) national-level priorities that may not sufficiently converge with SNG priorities (Soanes et al. 2017). This assessment pertains to all local actors but is likely to also reflect the limitations of SNG—on top of the aforementioned possibility that national rules could rule out or pose obstacles to external direct funding to SNGs.

The poor fiscal management capacities of many SNGs also show up in the inadequacy of data on local adaptation spending and bear negatively on the ability of SNGs to access climate funds. In countries that do not use climate change-specific budget codes in their expenditure tracking systems, tracking climate expenditure is difficult except when transfers are conditional to climate actions. The issue of climate expenditure tracking gets more complex when climate actions are mainstreamed in development investments at the local level (OECD 2019a). Efforts to track climate-related expenditure at the local level are hampered by factors such as difficulty in identifying the incremental expense of mainstreaming adaptation in a planned investment and lack of uniformity in the fiscal practices across sectors (see also Section III.B).

At least one international funder has tried to marry climate finance with capacity building. The United Nations Capital Development Fund designed and implemented the Local Climate Adaptive Living Facility (LoCAL) (Box 11), which seeks to align its support with decentralization systems and the intergovernmental structures of partner countries as well as the content of the NDC and SDG national priorities. It aims to institutionalize the successful results of piloted activities and processes and ensure the sustainability of investments made. LoCAL's efforts to connect partner countries with other climate funding mechanisms incentivize countries to support subnational and local levels to improve climate resilience.

Box 11: The Local Climate Adaptive Living Facility of the United Nations Capital Development Fund

The LoCAL mechanism of the UNCDF provides performance-based climate resilience grants to local governments in least developed countries to finance adaptation interventions. LoCAL works with the lowest or second lowest tier governments and small urban settlements. In Asia and the Pacific, the program has been active in Bangladesh, Bhutan, Cambodia, the Lao People's Democratic Republic, Nepal, and Tuvalu.

Performance-based climate resilience grants cover the additional costs of adaptation and making local development climate-resilient. The grants complement regular transfers to local government and differentiate themselves by including a set of minimum conditions, performance measures, and a menu of eligible investments that are aligned with national priorities. Performance measures are applied through an annual assessment to incentivize local governments to meet climate change adaptation objectives. The measures selected are informed by local climate risk assessments. The assessment is used to adjust the level of funding made available to the local government year to year as well as to identify the technical and capacity-building support needed. If local governments do not meet the minimum conditions, capacity gaps are identified and related capacity support is provided in part through LoCAL. These interventions help local governments better assess climate risks and vulnerabilities and integrate climate change adaptation into their planning and budgeting processes.

LoCAL is aligned with national climate change and decentralization strategies, NDCs, and NAPs, thus localizing the commitments of the Paris Agreement and achievement of the climate-related SDGs. It operates in distinct phases. The design phase focuses on engaging national, SNG, and key stakeholders, collecting and analyzing the information needed to design the program and to define the key elements of the LoCAL mechanism (flow of funds, grant allocation formula, minimum conditions, performance measures, menu of eligible investments, etc.). The first phase pilots the grants in two to four local governments. In the second phase, this is extended from 5 to 10 local governments, allowing for a more confident drawing of lessons and documented demonstrations of the grant mechanism's effectiveness. In the third phase, scaling-up and national rollout of LoCAL is expected.

The program challenges include maintaining flexibility to adjust the program to country-specific circumstances and pursue country-relevant adaptation goals while ensuring LoCAL standards are maintained and institutionalized. Also, low capacities of local governments in partner countries call for investment to safeguard effectiveness.

LoCAL = Local Climate Adaptive Living Facility, NAP = National Adaptation Plan, NDC = nationally determined contribution, SDG = Sustainable Development Goal, SNG = subnational government, UNCDF = United Nations Capital Development Fund.

Source: United Nations Capital Development Fund. 2017. Financing Local Adaptation to Climate Change; Experiences with Performance-Based Climate Resilience Grants.

As SNG experience with climate change action is gained, and success is made evident, global funds may assess their risk differently and work harder to establish easier access to these funds. In the meantime, SNGs will need to maximize domestic government and nongovernment sources to pilot approaches and make their case for more authority and resources, as this will remain the backbone of their funding beyond local taxes.

B. Accessing Transnational Networks Supporting Subnational Government Climate Change Action

In addition to funds, SNGs are much in need of technical support, and often this need outstrips what national actors can provide. SNGs, particularly larger cities and regions, have made good use of transnational networks to further their climate change governance (Hsu et al. 2020). Several networks relevant to SNGs have been established. ICLEI's Transformative Actions Program and C40's Cities Finance Facility were created to address the financing and capacity gaps noted at SNG level. The support provided helps local and regional governments develop robust and bankable projects ready for financing and implementation by connecting them with the right partners, experts, and project preparation tools.

A transnational connection can also help put forward the interests of SNGs toward climate change policy-setting bodies. United Cities and Local Government has joined with other organizations under the Local Authorities Major Group,[19] undertaking advocacy for all SNGs around a universal agenda (like responding to climate change). Specifically, the group has called for (LAMG 2022):

- a renewed, more inclusive, multilateral system based on ownership, co-creation, and peace, including and engaging local and regional governments and their representative associations in all stages of decision-making;
- leveraging linkages between the New Urban Agenda and the universal development agendas to ensure service delivery, and coordination among spheres of government to accelerate their implementation; and
- rethinking fiscal architecture and strengthening local finance to achieve the universal development agendas.

However, realizing these suggested initiatives very much depends on resources provided by international bilateral and multilateral/global funders.

[19] The Local Authorities Major Group brings together international networks and organizations that represent local and subnational governments from all continents in the world.

V. Addressing Subnational Government Capacity in Climate Change Governance

A. Proactive Communities Through Subnational Government Leadership

Addressing climate often requires choices to be negotiated (e.g., consumption patterns, higher costs, change in resource use, stringent standards, and relocations) for benefits that are unlikely to accrue entirely, or even largely, within the tenure of the elected government. The need to show tangible results within election cycles can deter relevant actions at the subnational level in developing countries and regions with fiscal resource constraints, where more immediate employment, development, and economic growth issues gain precedence. Regional/local leaders must cater to constituents' perceived/voiced short-term needs while eyeing actions geared toward sustainability. Support for climate change action can be found among any diverse population but citizens and organizations will perceive its desirability and cost in line with their lived experience and mindsets.

Political institutions, as gatherers of citizens' needs and wants, have established cultures and relationships that can resist change. Historical trajectories of development, past experiences of disaster events, the pressure of conflicting demands on limited resources, and community perceptions are some factors that influence the positioning of climate issues in agenda setting at different government levels. To break through some of the inertia and local rigidities in thinking requires leadership and, ideally, regional/local leadership that is attuned to the local context. These leaders need sufficient legitimacy and citizen support to take some risks. The population cannot be too riven by social divisions to prevent collaboration, or patience in waiting one's turn when resources are limited and phased rollouts are necessary. Moreover, leaders' role in political parties and their control of neighboring SNG or higher-level government posts of influence represent a factor that can facilitate local leadership or blunt it. Astute regional/local leaders will be aware of these contextual challenges and opportunities, anticipating their constituents' motivations and resistance to climate action.

Regional/local leaders need to bring to public roles skills that enable action on climate change. Adapting to climate change requires flexibility to redirect resources from activities threatened by climate change and support dependent populations to adopt new ones. Negotiating tradeoffs, incentivizing shifts, and enabling change requires communication, confidence, trust building, and risk taking. This combination of factors is not easy for elected officials to garner or to pass on in some measure to their bureaucracies. The tradeoffs in choosing climate-sensitive development over the cost of shorter-term economic gains need to be deliberated upon collectively at the subnational level. The risks, fears, and resultant reluctance need to be considered, and efforts must be made to build consensus even where there are uneven benefits across citizens and groups. Leaders need to be inspirational and lead by example, motivating citizens with visions of what even small SNGs can accomplish when volunteers, own-SNG resources, and well-targeted higher-level grants can be integrated into initiatives, as shown in the case of Odanthurai *panchayat* (village council) in southern India (Box 12).

Box 12: Odanthurai Village—Progressive Leadership Enabling Adaptation and Mitigation Actions

Odanthurai is located on the foothills of the Western Ghats, 40 kilometers from Coimbatore city in southern India. It is the first village in its region to incorporate wind, solar, and biogas energy into its community. It has set up a wind energy plant that can produce 350 kilowatts of electricity. Each home in this town also has a solar panel. It produces electricity for its own needs and also sells it to the Tamil Nadu Electricity Board, earning the community ₹20 lakh (around $25,000) annually in return.

When farmer Kasiviswanathan Shanmugam was elected president of the local government, he became invested in developing the community and the village. Under his leadership, the *panchayat* (village council) decided to explore tapping water from a perennial river close by. In 1999, the panchayat accessed a government-sponsored drinking water scheme, where 10% of the contribution was to be from the community and 90% from the Government of India. The community contributed ₹0.5 million ($5,500) and received ₹4.8 million ($590,000) from the government. In a year, the villages under the panchayat became water-independent.

The panchayat installed 500 streetlights and new motors for water lifting, filtering points, and booster stations for the drinking water plant. This had the effect of making electricity about 60% of the council's expenses. The increased bills spurred the panchayat to explore alternate energy options. To operate the local drinking water plant, a 9-kilowatt biomass gasifier system run on wood waste was installed. The gasifier cut pumping costs by almost 70% (this was discontinued at a later stage when the cost of wood waste rendered gasifier operations uneconomical). For streetlights, a 2-kilowatt solar system was installed. The success of biogas and solar energy bolstered interest in exploring alternatives for electricity.

The panchayat president convinced members to invest in a 350-kilowatt windmill, located 140 kilometers away in a wind farm owned by private renewable energy company Suzlon. Finance was accessed through a bank loan. This changed the economic dynamics of the area dramatically and led to its all-round development. Every month, the panchayat received an annual income of ₹1.9 million by selling surplus energy to the state electricity board and repaid ₹1.65 million annually as installments to the bank.

In the Odanthurai case, the economic motivation drove the local government to seek alternate energy options and explore funding arrangements. As is often the case, the activism of a leader of the local government sparks volunteerism and enables collective solution seeking. Success also lies in the ability of the local government to ensure convergence of different state subsidies and state-sponsored development programs and to leverage resources with a percentage contribution from the community as cofinance. Finally, the partnerships that the local government could forge with the private wind farm company, as well as the bank, serve as evidence of the critical role non-state actors can play in enabling transformation pathways.

Source: S. Balasubramanian. 2018. Odanthurai Uses Renewable Energy for All-Round Development. *India Climate Dialogue*. 13 June.

Just as leaders can exert a positive influence on citizens in climate change action, leaders and officials are in turn assessed for their ability to respond in anticipation of or consequent to a climate-related calamity. Elected leaders can be voted in or out based on their performance in terms of preparedness, quality of response, and effectiveness in the rehabilitation of affected communities. This pushes SNGs to weigh the tradeoffs between enabling short-term economic results and medium-term environmental protection and disaster prevention (Christoplos 2016). This sensitivity to local electors is missing where officials are appointed by higher levels of government, or where appointed officials dominate decision-making, relegating elected councils to rubberstamping decisions made by the appointed executives largely oriented to their national-level masters.

Regional/local leaders also need to weigh the benefits of cooperation with neighbors or higher-level government, versus undertaking projects where they can claim most of the success. Cooperation adds complexity and means sharing the credit for ultimate success. This is the hallmark of mature leadership, but political party allegiance and other factors sometimes get in the way of more strategic and long-term choices.

Platforms can be set up for the exchange of experience and know-how between communities/SNGs, or even between these and communities/SNGs in other regions. They can also seek to facilitate coalitions that potentially overcome resistance and spur action. One example of a platform to enhance SNG sharing of experiences is the Subnational Climate Action Leaders Exchange. This aims to leverage multilevel governance to significantly accelerate progress on subnational climate action, in part through showcasing the efforts of leading cities, states, and regions and facilitating peer-to-peer exchange and capacity building. It is focused on cutting methane emissions from waste and targets 40 SNGs around the world (WRI nd). It should be possible to foster similar approaches within all countries in Asia and the Pacific.

Forward-looking leaders at regional and local levels seek to build awareness of climate change threats and possible responses in the population, as seen in the case in Box 12 for the panchayat leader in promoting renewable energy. Regional and local institutions, like universities, civil society, and religious and philanthropic organizations can reach out to help in this work (see the case of universities in Indonesia in Box 13). Additionally, SNGs have the chance to link with transnational organizations that are focused on education, mobilization, and advocacy around climate change themes. These often seek to partner with local actors to provide proof of concept that can subsequently be offered as appropriate models for upscaling to national/regional levels of government.

A review of adaptation-related literature reveals that research on local adaptive actions has focused significantly on community-based adaptation. This is a valuable contribution, making a sound case for citizen participation in climate policymaking and solution seeking. The research has raised deliberated principles, tools, guidelines, and methodologies to enable citizen engagement in climate-related decision-making. However, this body of research can benefit greatly by extending its inquiry to the efficacy of formal arrangements of governance at the local level in multilevel governance systems. This includes the scope of action allowed in functional assignment and resources made available to SNGs. It also means helping SNGs recognize what communities can do with good leadership in place and how communities can be assisted by SNGs or by actors that are facilitated by SNGs.

B. Fostering Subnational Governments' Capacity to Address Climate Change

As investments in climate change action gain in ambition, the capacities of SNGs will prove critical to achieving scale and quality. Given that lower-level SNGs are the first responders to climate change effects, strengthening capacities at these levels is critical. Governments are constantly required to make choices on development pathways that balance the interests of local communities with the imperatives climate change poses at the local level. These imperatives could be in the form of adhering to new standards and protocols in infrastructure creation and services provisioning, climate-sensitive ecosystem management, land zoning, etc. The issues relating to capabilities and capacities of SNGs gain greater relevance in managing climate impacts owing to information asymmetries, uncertainty, frequency, the scales of operation demanded, and the high level of coordination required. The capacity issue also relates to evidence gathering on localized climate impacts, documenting local and indigenous knowledge, sharing good practices, and contributing to a body of experiential knowledge on climate impact.

Disaggregating National Determined Contributions to Greenhouse Gas Emission Reduction to Discern Subnational Government Roles

The need for capacity-building support for climate action is acknowledged by the setting up of the Paris Committee on Capacity-Building, which aims to bring coherence across diverse international capacity-building efforts. Its 2019 report noted that capacity gaps and needs were identified in adaptation in the areas of agriculture, coastal zone management, disaster risk reduction, energy, health, infrastructure, and water resources, as well as in mitigation in the areas of agriculture, energy, forestry, transport, and waste (UNFCCC 2019). Most of these sectors or issues fall under the jurisdiction of SNGs, or potentially could if a sensible functional assignment were put in place.

SNGs need to be supported in claiming their roles in climate change action that align with the always-evolving intergovernmental relationships—particularly functional assignment. For instance, in the case of Viet Nam, a starting point could be the NDC commitments to reduce GHG emissions. Currently, the NDC report lists these without providing any explanation of how Viet Nam's SNGs will fit in the effort to address these areas. Table 6 provides a tentative linkage that (once confirmed by stakeholders) could place the multilevel effort on a stronger footing (a full assignment of functions would be more specific). This is not a straightforward exercise in Viet Nam, as the assignment of functions is not clear (and is conducted through annual budget documents rather than stable lists of functions delineating the sector/service). Sometimes, functions that would be expected to be local responsibilities are still being exercised by the central level or are underfunded (UCLG and OECD 2016). For this reason, such an exercise would be valuable, allowing all levels of government to see clearly where their contribution must be made.

Similar efforts are needed on the adaptation side, with a bottom-up approach being even more important than in the case of the curbing of emissions, which has a more fixed model that needs national disaggregation. For adaptation, the specific conditions and risks felt at the local level would guide the development of a climate change action agenda, ideally to be integrated into the regular planning.

Table 6: Scope of Viet Nam's Nationally Determined Contribution as It Might Relate to Subnational Government Functions

Scope of Viet Nam's Nationally Determined Contribution (2022) Commitments to Reduce Greenhouse Gas Emissions	Level of Government with Possible Function (Sector Scope)			
	Central	Province/City	District	Village
Energy (emissions from fuel combustion) - Energy industry - Industrial production and construction - Transportation - Others: household, agriculture, services and trade	Energy industry; industrial production and construction; transportation	Energy industry	Agriculture	Household
Agriculture/rumen digestion - Organic fertilizer management - Rice cultivation	Organic fertilizer management; rice cultivation	Organic fertilizer management	Rice cultivation	Rice cultivation
Land use, land use change, and forestry - Forest land - Cultivation land - Grassland - Wetland	Forest land	Cultivation land; grassland; wetland	Cultivation land; grassland; wetland	Cultivation land
Waste - Landfills - Material production from solid waste - Domestic and industrial wastewater treatment	Material production from solid waste	Domestic and industrial wastewater treatment	Landfills	Landfills
Industrial processes - Construction materials - Chemical industry - Hydrofluorocarbon consumption	Construction materials; chemical industry; hydrofluorocarbon consumption	Not applicable	Not applicable	Not applicable

Sources: Socialist Republic of Viet Nam (2022) and author's judgment based on international practice as suggested for example in OECD (2019b).

Involving SNG in NDC and NAP Processes

National governments have rightly taken the lead in framing climate change action, for unitary and federal states. They have been supported by various global/international bodies in shaping their NDCs and NAPs. However, these have varied in their quality and level of disaggregation. SNGs may have only a peripheral or token role in the formulation of the NDC/NAP. Figure 3 sketches out the case of the Philippines as sketched out in the NDC implementation plan. Here, the local government units (LGUs) are mentioned as being involved in the Technical Working Group, but it is not clear how institutionally this is to happen. There is no specific mention of the local government associations in the scheme. These could play an important role in aggregating LGU views and commitments. The plan acknowledges that LGUs will need to be involved in the delivery of projects in transport, electric vehicle charging locations, and waste management and sewerage. It commits to identifying responsibilities, capacities, and needs at the LGU level, leaving the details to be developed later. Such tentative steps suggest LGUs are not in the thick of the national policy and planning of climate change action in the Philippines, raising questions regarding the pathway to disaggregating and implementing the policies and measures that constitute the NDC. Moreover, the link between local NAPs, which are being undertaken by many LGUs (spurred by the Climate Change Act of 2009), and the national NAP are unlikely to emerge strongly.

Figure 3: Partnership in Transparency. 2022 Preparation of the Philippine Nationally Determined Contribution

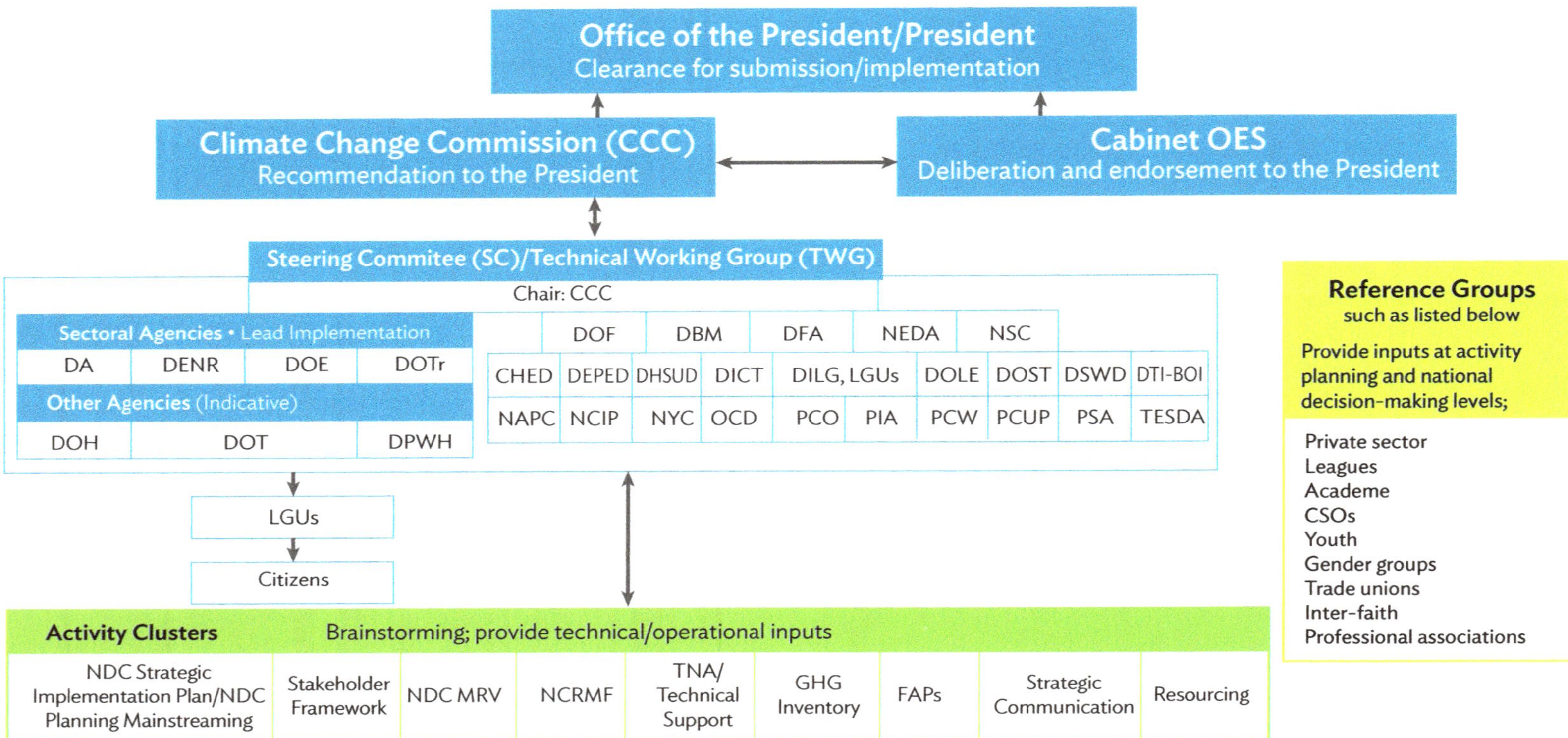

CHED = Commission on Higher Education; CSO = civil society organization; DA = Department of Agriculture; DBM = Department of Budget and Management; DENR = Department of Environment and Natural Resources; DEPED = Department of Education; DFA = Department of Foreign Affairs; DHSUD = Department of Human Settlements and Urban Development; DICT = Department of Information and Communications Technology; DILG = Department of the Interior and Local Government; DOE = Department of Energy; DOF = Department of Finance; DOH = Department of Health; DOLE = Department of Labor and Employment; DOT = Department of Tourism; DOTr = Department of Transportation; DPWH = Department of Public Works and Highways; DSWD = Department of Social Welfare and Development; DTI-BOI = Department of Trade and Industry Board of Investments; FAP = foreign-assisted project; GHG = greenhouse gas; LGU = local government unit; NAPC = National Anti-Poverty Commission; NCIP = National Commission on Indigenous Peoples; NCRMF = National Climate Risk Management Framework; NDC = nationally determined contribution; NDC MRV = NDC = Nationally Determined Contribution Measuring; Reporting, and Verification; NEDA = National Economic and Development Authority; NSC = National Security Council; NYC = National Youth Commission; OCD = Office of Civil Defense; OES = Office of the Executive Secretary; PCO = Presidential Communications Office; PCUP = Presidential Commission for the Urban Poor; PCW = Philippine Commission on Women; PIA = Philippine Information Agency; PSA = Philippine Statistics Authority; TESDA = Technical Education and Skills Development Authority; TNA = Technology Needs Assessment.

Source: Philippines NDC Implementation Plan (2023).

National governments and SNGs need to be supported to work together effectively to give the analysis underpinning the NDC/NAP more depth, disaggregation, and stakeholder awareness and commitment. This could be done through various approaches, including:

- closely involving SNGs and their associations in the NDC/NAP analysis;
- involving regional research bodies in the analysis;
- holding well-moderated multistakeholder events to firm up the analysis, conclusions, and agenda for mitigation and adaptation;
- providing joint training to key planners/researchers involved in the NDC/NAP at various levels of government to unify perceptions and ways of working together;
- linking SNG representatives with international organizations to strengthen their capacity on an ongoing basis; and
- encouraging NDC/NAP products that identify SNG roles and resources more clearly.

At SNG level, too often neglected in capacity building for climate governance, the pattern must be shifted from the typical socialization conducted by the national level (ad hoc, uniform in message, and generic forms of awareness raising)—focused on already prepared policies and plans—to engagement that heeds the aspirations and conditions of SNGs and local stakeholders. Capacity-building needs in this context call for at a minimum:

- strengthening coordination across the range of sectors implicated in SNG action;
- undertaking robust needs assessments;
- assisting in identifying financing sources; and
- accessing data or forming partnerships for better data (e.g., with academia) to undertake better planning.

This kind of capacity-building work does not need to be tightly connected to the NDC/NAP cycle. Ideally, more permanent efforts can be set in motion, that then can be tapped when the nationally driven opportunities present themselves. The linkages being formed in Indonesia's regions around the broad SDGs can be one model (Box 13); climate change action could well be subsumed under the SDG umbrella or have its own focus.

Organizational challenges at SNG level are widely recognized, affecting the discharge of all functions. It is often difficult for SNGs to attract and retain capable staff in most sectors and in research/planning functions. Attracting high-quality staff to support climate actions is even more difficult given the multisector scope of climate change. The lack of financial resources also tends to make capacity-building efforts episodic and insufficiently well designed. Finally, there is a lack of a comprehensive monitoring and review framework that could guide further investment in long-term capacity building.

Also, as countries strengthen NDC and NAP preparation, bottom-up planning and consultation processes can serve as a means of building institutional capacity across sectors and levels of government. The process of goal setting, data collection and interpretation, and consultatively arriving at commitments can serve to raise awareness and contribute to strengthened capacities. To further capitalize on the opportunities, preparation processes need to be followed by actions on the capacity gaps identified. For this, engagement and involvement of the training institutions designated as nodal capacity-building agencies for subnational and local governments need to be engaged more

Box 13: University Centers for the Sustainable Development Goals in Indonesia

As of July 2023, 38 centers for Sustainable Development Goals (SDGs) have been established in Indonesia, with the Ministry of National Development Planning (Bappenas) and the United Nations Development Programme backstopping this growth using the national academia SDG platform. Bappenas expects higher learning institutes in Indonesia to bolster their active collaboration on sustainable development issues, including in integrating SDGs into curricula, research, and dissemination of SDG-related public policy papers that will stimulate public discussion in seeking SDGs solutions.

Each of the university SDG centers operates according to its own model and focus. The national academia platform allows academics/SDG centers to share evidence-based SDG policy recommendations across the academic community and beyond.

The universities are spread across the archipelago, covering most provinces with one or more centers. These centers engage with subnational governments and relevant stakeholders in research and pilot projects designed to find solutions to achieving the subnational governments. Involving universities in pilot projects, if successful, is expected to trigger a snowball effect as other actors emulate these activities, leading possibly to transformative changes. Co-created solutions and knowledge, when disseminated by universities across broad stakeholders, have the potential to drive actions beyond the initial scope of pilot areas.[a]

[a] D. Agusdinata. 2002. The Role of Universities in SDGs Solution Co-Creation and Implementation: A Human-Centered Design and Shared-Action Learning Process. *Sustainability Science.* 17. pp. 1589–1604.

Source: R. Setiadi, E. Rapp, and G. Ferrazzi. 2019. The Role of the East Java Innovation Hub in Fostering Good Local Governance. *The Governance Brief.* Asia Development Bank, Issue 37.

comprehensively. As in the case of the SDGs network of university centers seen in Box 13, SNGs need to reach out to existing institutions to accompany them in key undertakings, particularly in the early stages of capacity building and climate action. Box 14 presents a case from Philippines where the opportunity of preparing local climate change action plans was leveraged to undertake a needs assessment of diverse stakeholders to evaluate preparedness and address capacity issues, again in a partnership with a nearby university.

Assessing Subnational Government Performance in Climate Change Action

Assessing the success of SNGs in climate change action is critical to improving their performance. As SNGs vie for resources nationally and globally, they will need to demonstrate success. The assessment can be driven by various actors and interests, but it should have a meaningful element of bottom-up monitoring, evaluation, and learning mechanisms to raise local perspectives.

The IPCC elaborates on three uses of metrics for assessing adaptation that apply to every level of governance: determining the need for adaptation, assessing the process of implementing adaptation, and measuring the effectiveness of adaptation. Metrics related to the need for adaptation would attempt to assess vulnerability. One of the key challenges in applying the IPCC approach is the challenge of defining adaptation initiatives; this will need to be addressed, differentiating adaptation from mainstream development interventions. Second, the challenge of attribution must be faced—particularly when the implementation period is long (IPCC 2014).

Box 14: Capacity Assessment for Local Climate Change Action Plan in Aurora, Philippines

Recognizing the grave risks posed by climate change, the Philippines passed the Climate Change Act in 2009. This stipulates the involvement of local government units (LGUs) as frontline agencies in the formulation, planning, and implementation of local climate change action plans (LCCAPs). All 1,489 municipalities and 145 cities in the Philippines need to prepare these plans. Provincial governments are to provide technical assistance, enforcement, and information management in support of municipal and city climate change action plans. These action plans are to be updated regularly to capture conditions.

Aurora Province in the Philippines is situated on Luzon Island and faces the Pacific Ocean, with no barriers to shield it from typhoons. The average monthly rainfall is 275 millimeters. It is highly vulnerable to sea level rise and coastal flooding and livelihood activities (farming, fishing, and tourism) are highly dependent on natural resources that are being adversely affected by climate change impacts (e.g., flooding, sea level rise, and landslides). Recognizing the gravity of the situation and seizing the opportunity presented by way of formulating the LCCAP, the Provincial Government of Aurora partnered formally with the University of the Philippines Los Baños to gain technical assistance in the formulation of the LCCAP. The provincial LGU of Aurora allocated additional funds for related capacity building of its personnel.

As an input to the LCCAP preparation, a comprehensive assessment of the strengths and challenges of LGUs in undertaking climate actions was undertaken. The areas of assessment included (i) enabling conditions to perform the assigned tasks; (ii) access to relevant information, institutional data, and information organization; (iii) capacity to make decisions in uncertain times while adhering to principles of good governance (transparency, accountability, responsiveness, etc.); (iv) awareness on climate issues, and capacity to generate, exchange, and apply the latest research, information, etc.; and (v) preparedness with knowledge, resources, and actions to avert or manage the impact of a disaster event. Each of the areas had between 15 and 20 parameters, which researchers assessed on a 5-point Likert scale. The Participatory Risk and Vulnerability Assessment allowed the research team to absorb knowledge of the local climate and disaster risks and helped identify sectoral data gaps for each municipality.

The key strengths that contributed to an enabling environment for the LGUs included access to training and a reasonable level of horizontal cooperation; well-defined systems in planning and decision-making that the staff was conversant with; high awareness of climate change issues in general, and high awareness of potential impacts of climate-related risk events to respective sectors; clear emergency response systems that were widely known; and good networks to disseminate information in times of emergency. On the other hand, the key challenges, signified by relatively lower scores, related to low staffing strength; insufficient leveraging of funding from private and nongovernment sources; weak systems of data management and information sharing during staff turnover; weak incentivization of individual performance; insufficient watershed-specific climate data and risk assessments; and limited infrastructure facilities and equipment to strengthen preparedness and respond to emergencies.

While the results of the participatory self-assessment in the LGUs are relevant to improving institutional wherewithal to strengthen climate resilience, what is more significant is the way the LCCAP preparation process was used as an opportunity to rally diverse stakeholders to review resources and processes. The partnership with an academic institution is significant in aiding academic rigor in methodological and analytical aspects as well as enabling access to knowledge resources and extending networks of

continued on next page

Box 14 *continued*

cooperation. The analysis and assessment also served to sensitize the LGUs and stakeholders, build capacities, and identify areas of support and cooperation across sectors and across municipalities. It provided the basis for a more realistic LCCAP that benefited from shared knowledge of strengths and challenges. The range of parameters that were rated in each of the five aspects assessed was significant in bringing forth the multiple facets of institutional preparedness and cooperative functioning to respond to climate challenges.

Source: L. Grefalda et al. 2020. Building Institutional Resilience in the Context of Climate Change in Aurora, Philippines. Environmental Research. 186, July.

Establishing monitoring, evaluation, and learning systems to assess mitigation or adaptation outcomes is also hampered by limited data availability and poor baseline information. Localizing the assessment is important since the intensity of the climate event is location-specific, but this very characteristic makes data gathering challenging. This may be one reason for a lack of standardized measures. The methodology is still under development (Christiansen, Martinez, and Naswa 2018). Developing locally appropriate and context-specific indicator frameworks and adaptation metrics should respond to the data needs of local institutions and base themselves on the descriptions and assessments of vulnerabilities and resilience. Supporting SNGs to develop context-specific indicators that can be integrated into national monitoring systems requires making tradeoffs between capturing the specifics of local risks, actions, impacts, and standardization of metrics to enable comparisons and upward integration (Coger et al. 2021).

SNGs are likely to be invested in developing and applying monitoring systems only if they have the flexibility to make changes in procedures and implementation actions based on the emerging learnings from the local assessments. Investments in designing assessment systems need to be accompanied by approaches affording SNGs the flexibility to actively support decision-making and make mid-course corrections rather than serving only the purpose of upward accountability. For the design of monitoring, evaluation, and learning systems to be meaningful, these systems would need to serve downward accountability as well so the results create an impetus for discussion, deliberation, and priority setting that will affect the next set of actions.

Currently, few countries have helped their SNGs develop appropriate approaches to assess mitigation or adaptation efforts conducted at regional/local level. They are largely preoccupied with shaping national monitoring and evaluation frameworks at this stage. Some governments have expressed their intent to follow up national monitoring and evaluation system development with efforts to develop subnational components and harmonize the two components. Cambodia has expressed this intention and is being supported by Germany in this long-term effort (GIZ 2017).

VI. Conclusions and Recommendations

A. Conclusions

SNGs in Asia and the Pacific matter in the battle against climate change, and they are taking the initiative in many cases, linking with local communities and other groups domestically and internationally. In some countries, SNGs are heavily involved in disaster risk reduction and management and in climate change actions. Using the conceptual framework of fiscal decentralization, SNG initiatives can be assessed to discern whether they play a meaningful role, or could do so with changes in the framework.

An initial test of meaningful SNG roles is whether respective states (national executive government and legislatures) have formally assigned functions to SNGs that are closely bound with climate change action. These would be functions in key sectors where important mitigation and adaptation efforts are found (e.g., energy, agriculture, transport, land use planning). In some countries, decentralization/SNG frameworks are favorable in this respect; in others, policy frameworks are not well developed or are inconsistently implemented.

Currently, the finances made available for climate change action in Asia and the Pacific for SNGs are generally not well aligned with the SNGs' actual functions or their potential role. This is especially true for finance for adaptation and resilience, which lags significantly behind that provided for mitigation. This imbalance tends to introduce an urban bias. Large cities are also quicker off the mark as they rely less on intergovernmental transfers, which are often conditional and not dedicated to climate change action. Adding dedicated transfers for SNG climate change action promises to redress the financing shortfall somewhat, ensuring less financially capable SNGs become involved. But this approach needs to guard against diminishing climate change action by relegating it to a special concern, planned and funded outside of the main development expenditures that potentially have a large impact on climate change adaptation and mitigation.

Regardless of how resources are channeled to SNG, it is important to enhance national and SNG ability to track these climate change expenditures, to determine what gets funded over time and where, and the success of these expenditures against climate change objectives. Challenges of definitions, data availability, and reporting may frustrate the development of climate change expenditure tracking methodologies that are still nascent.

In planning climate change actions, the pattern noted in Asia and the Pacific, as elsewhere, is national governments taking the lead, forging national policies and plans (NDC/NAP) aligned with countries' commitments to global framework agreements (e.g., the UNFCCC, the SDGs). This national leadership role (of the executive and legislative branches) is understandable given the spatial reach of climate change impacts and the centralization of technical and financial resources that marks both unitary and federal state systems. But to make these national policies and plans operational it is necessary to ensure SNG participation in and ownership of these, and to disaggregate targets to SNG scale, vesting ownership of targets to SNGs, in conformity with the legal or potential roles of SNGs in the general development process and climate change governance in particular.

Getting decentralization right in terms of the core elements of fiscal decentralization mentioned above is key to maximizing the role of SNGs in climate change governance. Decentralization has proceeded to different degrees in Asia and the Pacific—with reversals in some cases. It will be important for countries committed to universal agendas to empower their SNGs to attain maximum effort. There is scope in the region for SNGs to be further empowered to take responsibility for key sectors and services relating to climate change. Further refinement of vertical and horizontal coordination through planning and organizational structures/mechanisms can help in gaining coherence in a multilevel governance context. Revenue assignments that match the function load can make SNG action meaningful. The ability to issue debt could help the stronger and larger SNGs access finances that match their ambitions in climate change governance. Intergovernmental grants dedicated to climate change action could spread to incentivize SNG spending on climate change measures.

A crucial challenge for SNGs in countries with inadequate intergovernmental finance mechanisms is to find supplementary sources. Many nongovernment organizations nationally and globally can step in to help close the financing gap. However, SNG access to national and global funds (including MDBs) for both finance and capacity development is impeded by capacity issues. Most global climate funds rely on proposal-based systems to attract and screen projects. The proposal threshold in data and quality for gaining access to these funds is high. The practice of establishing entities that are gatekeepers for global funds or entities, through accreditation schemes, can ensure capacity and help direct funds to the local level, However, the "distance" between these entities and diverse and far-flung SNGs can potentially skew the allocation of resources in ways that leave SNGs playing roles that do not reflect their potential or the legal assignment of functions. More attention is needed to crafting channels that are appropriate to the low capacity of many SNGs and reflect local conditions.

B. Recommendations

These recommendations, aimed particularly at national governments and MDBs working in Asia and the Pacific, focus on investments that could help SNGs play a larger role in enhancing their climate change governance:

Proponents of SNG climate change action in Asia and the Pacific should continue to support efforts and approaches that are already underway, expanding these and improving on methodology. These efforts include:

1. more standardized methodologies for GHG inventories at subnational levels, thus facilitating the disaggregation of national targets to SNG level;
   a. expanding the application of climate risk and vulnerability assessments at SNG scales and with SNG involvement;

b. planning and budgeting approaches that integrate climate change actions, including disaster risk reduction and management actions (rather than marginalizing climate change by treating it as a small and special concern);
c. fostering partnerships between SNGs, businesses, and civil society;
d. promoting inter-SNG cooperation on climate issues;
e. supporting pilot projects and demonstrations of innovative climate solutions;
f. creating dedicated climate change units or focal points within local administrations; and
g. providing capacity development centered on proven approaches that can serve as models, (e.g., building partnerships and participation in knowledge-sharing networks involving SNG).

2. National governments in Asia and the Pacific must contend with the lag in SNG expenditure data—in what SNGs are receiving and spending on climate change action. In the context of the conclusion of the Paris Agreement and shaping what is to follow, closing the gap in SNG financing for climate change action is crucial. A finance hub in Asia and the Pacific for SNGs linked to the OECD or UNDP finance hub initiatives, or freestanding, could expedite the generation of SNG climate change data that can underpin national and supranational policies on climate change financing. Priority areas would include:
   a. a more widespread and standardized approach to national and SNG budget tagging;
   b. disaggregated and grouped data by MDBs and national and global funds on what climate change funding is provided to national versus SNGs in the Asia and the Pacific. This should differentiate participation of SNGs from ownership/fund management (on-budget/on-treasury); and
   c. an analysis covering Asia and the Pacific on which countries, SNGs, and population groups are receiving climate change funding, and for which kind of activities (mitigation, adaptation, sector).

3. National governments should actively encourage SNGs to join national efforts to prepare or revise key climate change policies and plans, like NDCs and NAPs. This could be achieved in several ways, including:
   a. establishing multistakeholder forums that have meaningful SNG participation;
   b. working closer with national SNG associations;
   c. encouraging SNGs to prepare similar policies/plans to their scale that can be considered as inputs to the national level policies and plans; and
   d. involving facilitating entities (e.g., MDBs, civil society) with expertise and commitment to empowering SNG climate change governance.

4. National governments and supporting actors should intensify support to fiscal decentralization related to climate change governance, including:
   a. establishing clear roles and responsibilities for climate action across levels of government. This could include allowing more freedom of action (e.g., discretionary functions, general competence architecture rather than a limited positive list);
   b. developing mechanisms for regular coordination between national and subnational governments (e.g., on readiness to respond to disasters);
   c. integrating planning and budgeting across levels of government in the preparation of key policies and plans (e.g., in the preparation or updating of NDCs and NAPs); and
   d. boosting local taxes and bond issuing to help decarbonize and raise revenue for climate change action.

5. MDBs and national/global funds can craft more alternatives in involving SNGs and directing funds to them. This can be done in several ways, including:
   a. working closer with national SNG associations;
   b. forming more partnerships with global/transnational networks of SNGs or organizations advocating for SNGs; and
   c. making it easier for intermediary-level (state, region, province) SNGs to become NDAs or accredited entities that can directly manage funds and distribute funds to other SNGs.

6. National governments, SNGs, and development partners should invest further in policy research, evaluation, learning tools, and dissemination of success stories regarding climate change action in Asia and the Pacific, with balanced attention between urban and rural contexts. Knowledge partnerships in this effort will be crucial to attaining rigor and disseminating lessons.

Appendix

Status of Submissions to the United Nations Framework Convention on Climate Change from Countries in Asia and the Pacific

No.	Country	NDC (Last Version)	NAPA[a]	NAP[b]	AC[c]
1	Australia	4 (2022)			1 (2021)
2	Bangladesh	3 (2021)	1 (2005)		
3	Bhutan	2 (2021)	1 (2006)		
4	Brunei Darussalam	1 (2020)			
5	Cambodia	2 (2020)	1 (2007)	1 (2021)	
6	People's Republic of China	2 (2021)			1 (2021)
7	Cook Islands	1 (2016)			
8	Fiji	1 (2020)		1 (2018)	
9	India	2 (2022)			
10	Indonesia	2 (2021)			
11	Japan	4 (2021)			1 (2021)
12	Kiribati	1 (2016)	1 (2007)	2 (2020)	
13	Republic of Korea	3 (2021)			
14	Lao People's Democratic Republic	2 (2021)	1 (2009)		
15	Malaysia	2 (2021)			

continued on next page

Table *continued*

No.	Country	NDC (Last Version)	NAPA[a]	NAP[b]	AC[c]
16	Maldives	2 (2020)	1 (2008)		
17	Marshall Islands	3 (2020)			1 (2020)
18	Federated States of Micronesia	1 (2016)			
19	Mongolia	2 (2020)			
20	Myanmar	2 (2021)	1 (2013)		
21	Nauru	1 (2021)			
22	Nepal	2 (2020)	1 (2010)	1 (2021)	1 (2021)
23	New Zealand	1 (2021)			1 (2017)
24	Niue	1 (2016)			
25	Pakistan	3 (2021)			
26	Palau	1 (2016)			
27	Papua New Guinea	1 (2020)			
28	Philippines	1 (2021)			
29	Samoa	2 (2021)	2 (2005)		
30	Singapore	2 (2020)			
31	Solomon Islands	1 (2021)	1 (2008)		
32	Sri Lanka	3 (2021)		1 (2016)	
33	Thailand	1 (2020)			
34	Timor-Leste	1 (2017)	1 (2011)	1 (2021)	1 (2021)
35	Tonga	1 (2020)			
36	Tuvalu	1 (2016)	1 (2007)		

continued on next page

Table *continued*

No.	Country	NDC (Last Version)	NAPA[a]	NAP[b]	AC[c]
37	Vanuatu	3 (2022)	1 (2007)		
38	Viet Nam	2 (2020)			

AC = Adaptation Communication, NAP = National Adaptation Plan, NAPA = National Adaptation Programme of Action.

[a] NAPAs are for least developed countries to identify priority activities that respond to their urgent and immediate needs about adaptation to climate change. They use existing information and no new research is needed.

[b] NAPs are a means of identifying medium and long-term adaptation needs and developing and implementing strategies and programs to address those needs. The two overarching objectives of NAPs are to reduce vulnerability to the impacts of climate change by building adaptive capacity and resilience; and to integrate adaptation into new and existing national, sectoral, and subnational policies and programs, especially development strategies, plans, and budgets.

[c] An AC is a voluntary report prepared by countries that synthesizes and shares their priorities, efforts, needs, and lessons around adapting to climate change.

Source: Asia-Pacific Climate Change Adaptation Information Platform.

References

Adaptation Fund (AF). Annual Performance Report for the Fiscal Year 2023.

D. Agusdinata. 2002. The Role of Universities in SDGs Solution Co-Creation and Implementation: A Human-Centered Design and Shared-Action Learning Process. *Sustainability Science.* 17. pp. 1589–1604.

A. Andrés Rodríguez-Pose and M. Vidal-Bover. 2023. Decentralisation, Unfunded Mandates, and the Regional Response to the COVID-19 Pandemic. Working Paper. International Center for Public Policy.

Asian Development Bank (ADB). 2022. Mainstreaming Climate Resilience into Development Planning in the Kingdom of Cambodia. Technical Assistance Completion Report (TA 8179). Manila.

–––. 2023. Uzbekistan: Validation of the Country Partnership Strategy Final Review. Manila.

R. Bahl. 2018. Metropolitan City Finances in the Asia and Pacific Region: Issues, Problems and Reform Options. In T. Subhanij, S. Banerjee, and Z. Jian, eds. *Tax Policy for Sustainable Development in Asia and the Pacific.* ESCAP.

R. Bahl and J. Martinez-Vasquez. 2022. Perspectives in Fiscal Decentralization: Challenges and the Unfinished Agenda. *Canadian Tax Journal* (supp.) pp. 69–96.

S. Balasubramanian. 2018. Odanthurai Uses Renewable Energy for All-Round Development. *India Climate Dialogue*. 13 June.

L. Baumgartner, R. Carman, and Y. Liu. 2022. *The State of Climate Ambition, Regional Snapshot Asia and the Pacific*. UNDP.

M. Betsill and H. Bulkeley. 2006. Cities and the Multilevel Governance of Global Climate Change. *Global Governance*. 12. pp. 141–160.

R. Bhandary. 2024. The Role of Institutional Design in Mobilizing Climate Finance: Empirical Evidence from Bangladesh, Brazil, Ethiopia, and Indonesia. *PLOS Climate.* 3 (3). e0000246.

S. Bhatt et al. 2019. India: NAPCC Process Country Case Study. GIZ.

J. Boex and J. Martinez-Vazquez. 2005. The Determinants of the Incidence of Intergovernmental Grants: A Survey of the International Experience. Andrew Young School of Policy Studies Research Paper.

H. Bulkeley. 2010. Cities and the Governing of Climate Change. *Annual Review of Environmental Resources*. 35. pp. 229–253.

N. Canales and G. Savvidou. 2023. Three Major Gaps in Climate-Adaptation Finance for Developing Countries. SEI Perspective.

B. Carrasco, H. Rahemtulla, and R. Rohdewohld, eds. 2022. *Decentralization, Local Governance, and Localizing the Sustainable Development Goals in Asia and the Pacific*. ADB/Routledge.

Charities Aid Foundation (CAF). 2022. *World Giving Index 2022. A Global View of Giving Trends*.

T. Carter et al. 2021. A Conceptual Framework for Cross-Border Impacts of Climate Change. *Global Environmental Change*. 69. July.

L. Chakraborty. 2021. Mainstreaming Climate Change Commitments Through Finance Commission's Recommendations. Working Paper. NIPFP

L. Christiansen, G. Martinez, and P. Naswa. 2018. *Adaptation Metrics: Perspectives on Measuring, Aggregating, and Comparing Adaptation Results*. UNEP DTU Partnership.

I. Christoplos et al. 2016. Understanding Subnational Climate Governance. Findings from Nepal, Uganda, Vietnam and Zambia. Report. Danish Institute for International Studies.

C. Clar and R. Steurer. 2019. Climate Change Adaptation at Different Levels of Government: Characteristics and Conditions of Policy Change. *Natural Resources Forum*. 43. pp. 121–131.

Climate Change Commission. 2024. Climate Change Programs – People's Survival Fund (PSF).

Climate Investment Funds (CIF). 2024. Asia.

T. Coger et al. 2021. Tracking and Reporting Finance for Locally Led Adaptation to Climate Change. Working Paper. World Resources Institute.

J. Corfee-Morlot et al. 2009. *Cities, Climate Change and Multilevel Governance*. Environmental Working Paper. OECD.

A. Dazé, H. Price-Kelly, and N. Rass. 2016. Vertical Integration in National Adaptation Plan (NAP) Processes: A Guidance Note for Linking National and Subnational Adaptation Processes. IISD.

DeLOG (Development Partners Working Group on Decentralization and Local Governance). 2014. Participants' Kit: Enhancing Development Effectiveness for Decentralization and Local Governance.

Dinas Energy dan Sumber Daya Mineral. 2021. Penandatanganan LoA Indonesia – Denmark oleh Duta Besar Denmark dan Gubernur NTB Tentang Transisi Hijau dan Investasi di Sektor Energi Terbarukan. November.

A. Dinshaw et al. 2018. Mainstreaming Adaptation in Action: Case Studies from Two States in India. Working Paper. World Resources Institute.

A. Dzebo et al. 2019. Connections Between the Paris Agreement and the 2030 Agenda. The Case for Policy Coherence. Working Paper. SEI.

Economic and Social Commission for Asia and the Pacific (ESCAP). 2021. *Asia Pacific Disaster Report 2021.*

---. 2022. Raising NDC Targets with Enhanced Nature-Based Solutions with a Special Feature on Engagement of Children and Youth in Raising National Climate Ambition. *2022 Review of Climate Ambition in Asia and the Pacific.*

S. Eskander and S. Steele. 2019. Bearing the Climate Burden: How Households in Bangladesh Are Spending Too Much. Issue Paper. IIED.

S. Eskander et al. 2022. Still Bearing the Burden: How Poor Rural Women in Bangladesh Are Paying Most for Climate Risks. Working Paper. IIED.

G. Ferrazzi. 2023. Indonesia's Decentralized Approach to Achieving the Sustainable Development Goals. In B. Carrasco, H. Rahemtulla, and R. Rohdewohld, eds. *Decentralization, Local Governance, and Localizing the Sustainable Development Goals in Asia and the Pacific.* ADB/Routledge.

G. Ferrazzi and R. Rohdewohld. 2017. *Emerging Practices in Intergovernmental Functional Assignment.* Routledge.

M. Fouad. et al. 2020. Unlocking Access to Climate Finance for Pacific Island Countries. Departmental Paper. IMF Asia-Pacific and Fiscal Affairs Departments.

J. Friedmann and C. Weaver. 1979. *Territory & Function: The Evolution of Regional Planning.* University of California Press.

R. Ghimire and N. Chhetri. 2022. Challenges and Prospects of Local Adaptation Plans of Action (LAPA) Initiative in Nepal as Everyday Adaptation. *Ecology and Society.* 27 (4).

GIZ (German Agency for International Cooperation). 2017. Cambodia: The National Climate Change Monitoring & Evaluation Framework.

Global Environment Facility (GEF). 2024. Work Program for GEF Trust Fund.

Global Water Partnership. 2017. Nepal's Approach to Climate Change Adaptation with Local Adaptation Plans for Action (LAPAs): A Water Resource Perspective.

Government of Nepal. 2011. National Framework on Local Adaptation Plans for Action.

Green Climate Fund (GCF). 2024a. Readiness and Preparatory Support: Strengthening Capacities to Increase Resilience with the Formulation of an Inclusive National Adaptation Plan (MyNAP) for Malaysia.

---. 2024b. Approved GCF Project Preparation Facility Application for Building Flood Resilient Community Through Adaptive Livelihood and Runoff Management in Petanglong Area of Central Java Province of Indonesia (BRAVE) Project.

L. Grefalda et al. 2020. Building Institutional Resilience in the Context of Climate Change in Aurora, Philippines. *Environmental Research*. 186, July.

A. Hsu et al. 2020. ClimActor, Harmonized Transnational Data on Climate Network Participation by City and Regional Governments. *Sci Data*. 7. 374.

ICLEI – Local Governments for Sustainability. *2018. Cities and Regions Talanoa Dialogues: Leveraging Subnational Action to Raise Climate Ambition.*

---. 2021. Our Vision for a Sustainable Urban World. April.

Indonesia Climate Change Trust Fund (ICCTF). 2024. ICCTF Credential.

Intergovernmental Panel on Climate Change (IPCC). 2014. *Climate Change 2014: Synthesis Report.* Contribution of Working Groups I, II and III to the Fifth Assessment Report.

---. 2023. *Climate Change 2023: Synthesis Report.* Contribution of Working Groups I, II, and III to the Sixth Assessment Report.

---. 2024. Decisions Adopted by the Panel. Sixty-First Session of the IPCC. 27 July–2 August, Sofia, Bulgaria.

International Institute for Environment and Development (IIED). 2024. Principles for Locally Led Adaptation.

Kementerian Lingkungan Hidup dan Kehutanan. 2022. Menteri LHK Meminta Para Gubernur Untuk Pemahaman Bersama Tentang Perkembangan Perubahan Iklim Dan Karbon.

M. Liu, Y. Xiong, and Zhang, A. 2024. Can China's Cross-Regional Ecological Fiscal Transfers Help Improve the Ecological Environment?—Evidence from Hubei Province. *Land.* 13 (8).

Local Authorities Major Group (LAMG). 2022. 2022 United Nations High-Level Political Forum.

L. Loft, M. Gebara, and G. Wong. 2016. The Experience of Ecological Fiscal Transfers: Lessons for REDD+ Benefit Sharing. Occasional Paper 154. CIFOR.

J. Martinez-Vazquez. 2021. *Adapting Fiscal Decentralization Design to Combat Climate Change.* World Bank.

Ministry of Environment (Cambodia) and UNDP (United Nations Development Programme). 2011. *Cambodia Human Development Report: Climate Change and Local Action in Cambodia.*

E. Mitroliou. 2018. Data Speak Louder Than Words: Findings from an Initial Stocktake of Climate Change Adaptation and Urban Resilience Efforts. ICLEI/C40.

K. Mogelgaard et al. 2018. From Planning to Action: Mainstreaming Climate Change Adaptation into Development. Working Paper. World Resources Institute.

B. Naran et al. (2022). *Global Landscape of Climate Finance: A Decade of Data 2011-2020.* Climate Policy Initiative.

NDC 3.0 Navigator. 2024. Engaging Local and Regional Governments.

NDC Partnership. 2020. Engaging Subnational Governments in Climate Action – Lessons Learned from the NDC Partnership Support Unit. Insight Brief, March.

National Committee for Subnational Democratic Development (NDCC), 2023. Report on Results of the Evaluation of the Management, Administration and Implementation of Educational Function Transferred to the Municipal & District/Khan Administration. Supported by NCDDS and ISD/GIZ Programs.

National Council for Sustainable Development (NCSD). 2019. Mid-Term Review of Cambodia Climate Change Strategic Plan 2014 – 2023. Final Evaluation Report. Supported by CCCA and UNDP.

Organisation for Economic Co-operation and Development (OECD). 2019a. Financing Climate Objectives in Cities and Regions to Deliver Sustainable and Inclusive Growth. Environment Policy Paper. OECD.

---. 2019b. Making *Decentralisation Work: A Handbook for Policy-Makers.*

---. 2022a. Subnational Government Climate Expenditure and Revenue Tracking in OECD and EU Countries. Regional Development Paper.

---. 2022b. Aligning Regional and Local Budgets with Green Objectives: Subnational Green Budgeting Practices and Guidelines. Multi-level Governance Study.

---. 2022c. *Aggregate Trends of Climate Finance Provided and Mobilised by Developed Countries in 2013-2020.*

OECD and ADB. 2023. *Multi-Level Governance and Subnational Finance in Asia and the Pacific.* OECD Regional Development Paper.

Partnership in Transparency. 2022. Strengthening Community Level Climate Change Adaptation and Mitigation Actions: Indonesia's Climate Village Programme (ProKlim).

S. Patel et al. 2020. Good Climate Finance Guide: Lessons for Strengthening Devolved Climate Finance. Working Paper. IIED.

Practical Action. 2024. Enhancing Impact: Lessons from Nepal's Local Adaptation Plans of Action.

E. Rahman. 2019. Mengenalkan Skema Insentif Fiskal Berbasis Ekologi di Indonesia: TAKE, TAPE Dan TANE. The Asia Foundation.

R. Setiadi, E. Rapp, and G. Ferrazzi. 2019. The Role of the East Java Innovation Hub in Fostering Good Local Governance. *The Governance Brief*. Asia Development Bank, Issue 37.

R. Shaw, Y. Luo, and T. Sung. 2022. Asia. In IPCC. *Climate Change 2022: Impacts, Adaptation and Vulnerability*. Contribution of Working Group II to the Sixth Assessment Report.

P. Smoke. 2001. Fiscal Decentralization in Developing Countries: A Review of Current Concepts and Practice. Democracy, Governance and Human Rights Programme Paper. UNSRID.

M. Soanes et al. 2017. Delivering Real Change: Getting International Climate Finance to the Local Level. Working Paper. IIED.

Socialist Republic of Viet Nam. 2022. *Nationally Determined Contribution (NDC).*

L. Strauch, Y. Robiou du Pont, and J. Balanowski. 2018. Multi-Level Climate Governance in Vietnam. Bridging National Planning and Local Climate Action. adelphi.

Under2 Coalition. 2024. Next Generation Budgets.

United Cities and Local Governments (UCLG) and OECD. 2016. *Subnational Governments Around the World: Structure and Finance. A First Contribution to the Global Observatory on Local Finances.* October.

United Nations. 2015a. Transforming Our World: The 2030 Agenda for Sustainable Development.

---. 2015b. Sendai Framework for Disaster Risk Reduction 2015–2030.

---. 2023. *The Sustainable Development Goals Report.* Special Edition.

United Nations Capital Development Fund (UNCDF). 2017. Financing Local Adaptation to Climate Change; Experiences with Performance-Based Climate Resilience Grants.

United Nations Development Programme (UNDP). 2019a. *Knowing What You Spend: A Guidance Note for Governments to Track Climate Change Finance in their Budgets.*

---. 2019b. *Climate Public Expenditure and Institutional Review (CPEIR).*

---. 2022. Global Climate Public Finance Review.

United Nations Environment Programme (UNEP). 2022. *Too Little, Too Slow: Climate Adaptation Failure Puts World at Risk*. Adaptation Gap Report.

United Nations Framework Convention on Climate Change. 2015. The Paris Agreement.

---. 2019. National-Level Pilot Exercise on Capacity Gaps and Needs Related to the Implementation of Nationally Determined Contributions. Technical Paper.

United Nations Population Fund (UNFPA). 2023. Asia and the Pacific – Population Trends.

R. Weikmans and J. Timmons Roberts. 2019. The International Climate Finance Accounting Muddle: Is There Hope on the Horizon? *Climate and Development*. 11. pp. 97–111.

World Bank. 2022a. *Green Growth and Climate Change in Uzbekistan Policy Dialogue Series: A Compendium of Proceedings*.

---. 2022b. *Philippines Country Climate and Development Report*.

---. 2024. *Scaling Up Locally-Led Climate Action In Cambodia*. In collaboration with the Global Facility for Disaster Reduction and Recovery and the National Committee for Sub-National Democratic Development Secretariat.

World Resources Institute (WRI). nd. Subnational Climate Action Leaders Exchange.

World Wildlife Fund. 2020. How Cities Around the World Are Working Toward a Greener Future. *World Wildlife Magazine*. Summer.

C. Yap, C. Cociña, and C. Levy. 2021. The Urban Dimensions of Inequality and Equality. Gold VI Working Paper. UCLG and KNOW.

www.ingramcontent.com/pod-product-compliance
Lightning Source LLC
Chambersburg PA
CBHW041758220926
51847CB00014B/243
9789292773106